Productions of the Irish Theatre Movement, 1899–1916

Recent Titles in
Bibliographies and Indexes in the Performing Arts

The Hispanic Image on the Silver Screen: An Interpretive Filmography from Silents into Sound, 1898–1935
Alfred Charles Richard, Jr.

A Guide to Silent Westerns
Larry Langman

Censorship and Hollywood's Hispanic Image: An Interpretive Filmography, 1936–1955
Alfred Charles Richard, Jr.

A Guide to American Silent Crime Films
Larry Langman and Daniel Finn

Contemporary Hollywood's Negative Hispanic Image: An Interpretive Filmography, 1956–1993
Alfred Charles Richard, Jr.

Theatre at Stratford-upon-Avon, First Supplement: A Catalogue-Index to Productions of the Royal Shakespeare Company, 1979–1993
Michael Mullin

A Guide to American Crime Films of the Thirties
Larry Langman and Daniel Finn

An Index to Short and Feature Film Reviews in the Moving Picture World: The Early Years, 1907–1915
Annette M. D'Agostino, compiler

A Guide to American Crime Films of the Forties and Fifties
Larry Langman and Daniel Finn

Theatrical Design in the Twentieth Century: An Index to Photographic Reproductions of Scenic Designs
W. Patrick Atkinson

American Film Cycles: The Silent Era
Larry Langman

A Guide to Charlie Chan Films
Charles P. Mitchell

Productions of the Irish Theatre Movement, 1899–1916

A Checklist

Compiled by
Nelson O'Ceallaigh Ritschel

Bibliographies and Indexes in the Performing Arts, Number 24

GREENWOOD PRESS
Westport, Connecticut • London

Library of Congress Cataloging-in-Publication Data

Ritschel, Nelson O'Ceallaigh, 1959–
  Productions of the Irish theatre movement, 1899–1916 : a checklist / compiled by Nelson O'Ceallaigh Ritschel.
    p. cm.—(Bibliographies and indexes in the performing arts, ISSN 0742-6933 ; no. 24)
  Includes bibliographical references and index.
  ISBN 0–313–31744–5 (alk. paper)
  1. Theater—Ireland—20th century—Calendars. I. Title. II. Series.
PN2601.R58 2001
792'.09417'09041—dc21   00–049049

British Library Cataloguing in Publication Data is available.

Copyright © 2001 by Nelson O'Ceallaigh Ritschel

All rights reserved. No portion of this book may be reproduced, by any process or technique, without the express written consent of the publisher.

Library of Congress Catalog Card Number: 00–049049
ISBN: 0–313–31744–5
ISSN: 0742–6933

First published in 2001

Greenwood Press, 88 Post Road West, Westport, CT 06881
An imprint of Greenwood Publishing Group, Inc.
www.greenwood.com

Printed in the United States of America

The paper used in this book complies with the Permanent Paper Standard issued by the National Information Standards Organization (Z39.48–1984).

10 9 8 7 6 5 4 3 2 1

Contents

Preface	vii
Introduction	1
1899	5
1900	7
1901	9
1902	11
1903	15
1904	21
1905	25
1906	29
1907	33
1908	39
1909	47
1910	55

1911	65
1912	73
1913	81
1914	91
1915	99
1916	107
Works Cited	113
Index	115

Preface

THIS WORK LISTS as many productions of the first modern Irish theatre movement as is possible, starting in 1899 with the Irish Literary Theatre. While it is impossible to list every production, due to the numerous stage offerings by the many Gaelic League branches outside Dublin and the occasional tours by the major companies of the smaller cities, this is the most comprehensive list ever presented. Unlike previous lists that only partially numbered premieres, this work includes premieres and revivals. Revivals, as is no doubt revealed, often were as important as the premieres. Such information offers new insight into the major writers and the operation of the Abbey Theatre itself. For example, is it significant that Synge's plays were among the most revived at the early Abbey, despite their volatile receptions when premiered? Also we can gain further understanding of the political, cultural, and theatrical context of the major writers—thorough production histories are possible, as is an appreciation of the Abbey as a working, practical institution.

Nevertheless, this work's greatest contribution is the information that it brings to light on the entire Irish theatre movement. It is now possible to realize exactly how many theatres and writers were involved, offering credence to the movement's actor Maire Nic Shiubhlaigh's recollection that "Dublin was drama-mad in every sense of the word" (140). Indeed, as far as the urban centers were concerned, Ireland was drama-mad. There was a truly phenomenal movement that perhaps almost rivals the theatrical movement of Elizabethan-Jacobean England. The research that this work makes possible are enormous, and the surprises are indeed engaging.

One surprise is the revelation that there were *many* women dramatists (in addition to Gregory), who had their work performed. Sadly, there is little known of these writers, but now there is at least a record of their work and a possible starting point for further research.

This work, as comprehensive as it attempts to be, only covers the years 1899–1916, specifically ending in April 1916 at the time of the Easter Rising. This is due to the fact that Irish theatre after the Rising was greatly altered by the British martial law that was immediately in effect, and by the loss of many key theatre artists because of either death (fighting during the Rising or executions afterwards) or their incarceration due to their participation. Irish theatre did not really regain its footing until the emergence of Sean O'Casey, and by then the theatre fostered new and different agendas, as did most post World War I European theatre.

Since all of the theatres involved, except for the National Theatre Society Limited from 1905 on, were amateur enterprises, many productions were never advertised. Instead they relied on the radical press to kindly mention their schedules. Consequently, information on a few productions is indeed light. On the whole, very few productions were ever reviewed, and most of the plays were never published. The following primary sources were used to compile the list of productions: *The United Irishman* 1899–1906, *Sinn Fein* (weekly) 1906–1914, *Sinn Fein* (daily) 1909–1910, *The Freeman's Journal* 1899–1916, *Nationality* 1915–1916, *The Belfast Evening Telegraph* 1903–1905, and *The Workers' Republic* (second series) 1915–1916. All were radical newspapers except for *The Freeman's Journal* and the *Belfast Evening Telegraph;* the former was associated with the Home Rule movement while the latter was closer to Unionist interests. What separates the above radical papers from other such presses of the time was the value they placed on theatre—something that *The Freeman's Journal* shared. Arthur Griffith, editor of *The United Irishman,* both *Sinn Feins,* and *Nationality,* devoted great space to the non-commercial theatre presented in Dublin and throughout Ireland. As a consequence, many theatres, through either advertisements or space allowances, saw their scheduled productions in the pages of Griffith's papers (although less so with *Nationality* which Griffith did not own). The larger or more ambitious theatres like the National Theatre Society Limited and Cluithcheoiri na hEireann (Theatre of Ireland) regularly advertised in Griffith's papers and *The Freeman's Journal.* By the autumn of 1915 the labor weekly *The Workers' Republic,* edited by James Connolly for the Irish Transport and General Workers Union (ITGWU), ran regular ads for the increased productions of the Irish Workers' Dramatic Company; both the Theatre and paper were based in the ITGWU's Liberty Hall. As Connolly turned his agenda toward the nationalist camp, his little Theatre began to present productions on a weekly basis. In fact, the Irish Workers' Dramatic Company has the distinction of staging the last new play of the theatre movement—James Connolly's only play, *Under Which Flag.* This is perhaps appropriate since a significant number of playwrights and actors from the theatre movement marched from Liberty Hall in April 1916 into the Easter Rising.

The following entries are numbered chronologically, with each listing title and author first, followed by the producing theatre/organization, building, city, and dates. Most of the Irish theatre movement's theatres rented halls or theatre buildings. It is important to remember that the Abbey Theatre was specifically the name of the theatre building operated by the Irish National Theatre Society, which was reorganized into the National Theatre Society Limited in 1905. The Society frequently rented the Theatre to other organizations.*

I WISH TO ACKNOWLEDGE with great thanks Spencer Golub with whom I first discussed this project in 1994. The friendship and professional advice from Don Wilmeth has been most helpful for not only this project, but for others as well. Stephen Watt also deserves a warm acknowledgment as his encouragement of my work has meant a great deal.

The staff of the National Library of Ireland has been extremely helpful, as has the staff of the document/microfilm center of Boston College's O'Neill Library. Their patience and persistence in dealing with me is most appreciated.

I must also thank Brenda for her constant watch.

---

*A small number of production entries include a "(?)," denoting that specific information is either sketchy or incomplete.

Introduction

IRELAND HAS PROVIDED many contributions to theatre since the English Restoration, and today enjoys a superb if not curious reputation as a theatre-rich country—from Brian Friel to Christina Reid—yet prior to 1899 Ireland was void of a native theatrical tradition. Yes, Irish-born dramatists overshadowed their contemporaries in English theatre during the eighteenth century when actor Charles Macklin, with his Donegal roots, rivaled the great David Garrick in roles such as Shakespeare's Shylock. Macklin eventually returned to Dublin in 1762, specifically composing his Swiftian comedy *The True-Born Irishman* for the engagement. Even though this play might be construed as an example of Irish literature, and reflected the nationalism of Grattan's Parliament, the play was not part of a native Irish theatrical movement—at least not until it was revived and revised in 1910. While English theatre again reached its artistic pinnacle in the nineteenth century via Dublin-raised playwrights, namely George Bernard Shaw and Oscar Wilde, Ireland also produced a number of writers who dominated the century's popular venue of melodrama. The most noted, of course, was Dion Boucicault.

Although the prolific Boucicault wrote many melodramas on numerous subjects, he is perhaps best remembered for his Irish-based plays, including *The Colleen Bawn* (1860), *Arrah-na-Pogue* (1864), *The Shaughraun* (1875), and *Robert Emmet* (1884). Despite the fact that these dramas were written for London and New York, many consider them Irish plays, in the sense of a native drama. Support for such a conclusion can be found in public statements by the actor-playwright Boucicault himself, as in 1875: "It is the Irish character as misrepresented by the English dramatists that I convict as a libel" (qtd. in Grene 8). To counter this libel Boucicault, Nicholas Grene argues, created Irish heroic images like *The Colleen Bawn*'s Myles-na-Coppaleen and *The Shaughraun*'s Conn, who were designed to be "the essence of Irishness as it is manifested in fairs and funerals, wakes and weddings." Such characters, however, "came to be despised as stage-

Irishry, castigated for its inauthenticity, condemned for its ingratiating 'blarney' and 'bootlicking' " (Grene 14, 17). Nevertheless, the belief that Boucicault's Irish plays represented a native Irish drama is mostly due to the fact that his plays spawned additional such Irish melodramas from actor-manager-playwrights like Hubert O'Grady and the English-born J. W. Whitbread. Because Whitbread's and O'Grady's, and occasionally Boucicault's, Irish melodramas were frequently staged in Dublin's popular Queen's theatre in the late nineteenth-early twentieth century, many feel today that they served nationalist interests—and therefore should be considered Irish theatre. Stephen Watt argues that:

> The effect of such plays was to accelerate the development of nationalist consciousness among a general audience while supplying powerfully emotive stereotypes of patriotic heroes and heroines, cowardly informers, and villainous British officers. (Watt 479)

Certainly such plays at the Queen's did promote nationalism, hence an Irish agenda, for a primarily working-class audience. However, middle-class nationalists, the class that would produce the 1916 Easter Rising, rejected the Boucicault-type melodramas as Irish theatre. The Dublin amateur actor and nationalist theatre critic Frank Fay expressed his view of such theatre to W. B. Yeats in 1902:

> His [Whitbread's] theatre . . . is the shoddiest kind of melodrama and is only a little less harmful than the [English] music hall. His patrons are or ought to be nationalists but are of the music hall type, and they applaud the British flag as soon as the Irish. (qtd. in Hogan And Kilroy 31)

Fay, writing for the nationalist radical newspaper *The United Irishman,* waged a war against such theatre from 1899–1901 with a series of reviews and articles that seemingly extended from his conviction that Boucicault was a mere "master of commonplace stage-craft with nothing to say" (qtd. in Holloway 34). Of Whitbread's *Wolfe Tone* Fay writes: "we have not yet had a real . . . Irish drama, and the author of 'Wolfe Tone' cannot give us one. . . . It is neither more nor less than a well-constructed melodrama" (Fay 5). The key to the ardent nationalists' objection to this type of play had to do with the very form. Fay's colleague at *The United Irishman,* William Rooney, commented on Hubert O'Grady's plays: "[his] work is well in aim, but wretched and exaggerated in execution" (Rooney 1). Even James Connolly's *The Workers' Republic* weekly reviewed in 1915 another such melodrama by a newer Boucicault-type author, P. J. Bourke: "The play is such a terrible mixture of duels . . . climax and anti-climax, that it would be indeed, very difficult to . . . give an idea of what it was all about" (*"The Land She Loved" 3*). The style of melodrama, after all, was not an Irish form, but an English one. Lady Gregory, one of the principals who would indeed create a truly native Irish theatre, attended a revival in England of O'Grady's melodrama "The Fenian" in 1899:

> We went to "The Fenian" at the Imperial theatre close by—very funny—a Trinity lad the villain, in cap & gown, with a background of Ceylon *palm* trees! [Gregory's italics] Then a coast guard, an old woman from a cabin, a Fenian midnight meeting in a cave (or forest) where, in spite of secrecy, the band was playing Irish airs on brass instruments! Hubert O'-Grady the writer of the piece played the comic part very well, & it was very amusing on the whole. (Gregory 213)

Amusement for solely entertaining purposes was a main feature of such melodramas. J. W. Whitbread's *Wolfe Tone* (1898), for example, features two servants, Shane McMahon and Peggy Ryan, who deliver numerous comic exchanges. In Act II when no sherry is to be found for guests, Shane offers whiskey, prompting Peggy to slam a door in his face, to which Shane replies, "She say she's no Peg for me to hang me hat on" (Whitbread 205).

Such comedy from Shane and Peggy no doubt is an example of what Grene labels "stage-Irishy," leaving much to be desired by those who sought to re-image Ireland at the beginning of the twentieth century. A more immediate result of the melodramas' comedy, and other elements of the English form like the fantastical triumph of the hero, led to the creation of a certain audience. One contemporary described the audience of Dublin's Queen Theatre—shaped by the melodramas—as "Savages' . . . with whistling, chirping, chattering out loud, banging of doors, and stumbling in and out of the bar at the most inopportune moments" (qtd. in Hogan and Kilroy 65).

Indeed, how could such a theatre and drama seriously begin what the nationalist portrait painter John B. Yeats described as "the work of self-examination and self-accusation" of their country (2). By the end of the nineteenth century the need had arisen in Ireland, as part of its de-colonization process, to create a native theatre of its own, with its own forms and aesthetics. This commenced, of course, with the Irish Literary Theatre.

The Irish Literary Theatre, though not terribly prolific or successful on its own, gave rise to what would become by 1902 a phenomenal, wholly native, non-commercial Irish theatre movement. By 1916 this movement, an explosion of theatrical endeavors, would amass more than 1,100 productions of both premieres and revivals. This was surely a spectacular accomplishment given the country's non-existing theatre prior to May 1899. Even more spectacular was the movement's fostering of such crucial dramatists as John M. Synge, W. B. Yeats, and Lady Augusta Gregory—not to mention the establishment of the National Theatre Society Limited, or Abbey Theatre—a potent enterprise that deservedly can be ranked next to ventures like the Moscow Art Theatre. Nevertheless, given the enormity of this Irish theatre movement, the Abbey and its chief playwrights are only part of the story. In 1903 the Abbey's predecessor, the Irish National Theatre Society, fractured and formed the Cumann na nGaedhael Irish Theatre Company, the first of an almost innumerable number of splinter or smaller theatres that formed throughout Ireland during the next thirteen years—hence a movement. These theatres include (but are not limited to) the Players' Club, the Ulster Literary Theatre, the Cork National Theatre, Cliuthcheoiri na hEireann (Theatre of Ireland), the Cork Dramatic Club, the National Stage Society, the National Players Society, the Independent Theatre Company, the Irish Historical Players, the Pioneer Dramatic Society, the Leinster Stage Society, the Irish Theatre Company, the Irish Workers' Dramatic Company, and numerous Gaelic League Branch theatres. Together with the Abbey these theatres staged the works by writers such as Frederick Ryan, James Cousins, Edward Martyn, Henry Connell Mangan, Joseph Ryan, W. P. Ryan, Lewis Purcell, John O'Loughlin, Mary Costello, Johanna Redmond, Maire Ni Cinneide, E. Hamilton Moore, William Boyle, Norreys Connell, George Fitzmaurice, Alice Milligan, T.C. Murray, Padraic Colum, Seumas O'Brien, James Stephens, Eimar O'Duffy, Thomas MacDonagh, Padraic Pearse, Seumas O'Kelly, Margaret Pearse, James Connolly, W. F. Casey, Terence MacSwiney, Rutherford Mayne, Edward McNulty, and many more. Such theatres and playwrights, arguably pursuing political and/or cultural agendas, paved the way for Sean O'Casey and all the rest.

Obviously there has been a great deal of study directed toward this first modern theatre movement in Ireland. Nevertheless, many of the writers and theatres mentioned above have received little or no attention. This is due in part to the titans of the movement, who have warranted exhaustive study. Obviously, full knowledge of the movement can only increase one's understanding of the major playwrights and their theatre. However, a record of much of the movement has simply not been easily accessible—until now.

1899

1. *The Countess Cathleen* by W. B. Yeats. The Irish Literary Theatre, Antient Concert Rooms, Dublin: 8, 10, 12, 13 May 1899.

2. *The Heather Field* by Edward Martyn. Same theatre and location as above: 9, 10, 13 May 1899.

1900

3. *Maeve* by Edward Martyn. The Irish Literary Theatre, Gaiety Theatre, Dublin: 19 February 1900.

4. *The Last Feast of the Fianna* by Alice Milligan. Same theatre and location as above: 19 February 1900.

5. *The Bending of the Bough* by George Moore. Same theatre and location as above: 20 February 1900.

1901

6. *Tadg Saor (Freeman Man)* by Father O'Leary. Rosmore Gaelic League, County Cork (?): March 1901.

   Possibly this was the first play of the Theatre Movement performed in Irish.

7. *Tableaux Vivants* "Grand display of Gaelic History and Legendary Scenes." Inghinidhe na hEireann, Antient Concert Rooms, Dublin: 8, 9 April 1901.

8. *The Harp That Once* by Alice Milligan. Inghinidhe na hEireann, staged by Frank and William Fay, Antient Concert Rooms, Dublin: 26, 28, 30 August 1901.

   The scheduling of productions during Horse Show week was a tradition the Abbey Theatre would later continue.

9. *The Deliverance of Red Hugh* by Alice Milligan. Same theatre and location as above: 27, 29, 31 August 1901.

10. *Eilis agus Bhean Deirce (Lizzie and the Beggarwoman)* by P. T. Mac Fhionnlaioch (P.T. MacGinley). Same theatre and location as above: 27, 29, 31 August 1901.

    Reportedly, this play was performed earlier outside of Dublin, but its location and date are not known—often cited as the first play of the movement performed in Irish.

11. *Irish Tableaux Vivants.* Inghinidhe na hEireann, staged by Frank and William Fay, Antient Concert Rooms, Dublin: 31 August 1901.

   This production may have also been staged earlier in the week as a matinee with the above plays.

12. *Diarmuid and Grannia* by George Moore and W. B. Yeats. The Irish Literary Theatre, Gaiety Theater, Dublin: 21, 22, 23 October 1901.

13. *Casadh an tSugain (The Twisting of the Rope)* by Douglas Hyde. Same theatre and location as above, performed by the Keating Gaelic League branch, staged by William Fay (possibly with Frank Fay): 21 22, 23 October 1901.

1902

14. *Deirdre* by AE (George Russell). Acts I and II performed by W.G. Fay's amateur acting company, staged by Frank and William Fay, garden of George Coffey's home, 5 Harcourt Terrace, Dublin: 2, 3 January 1901.

15. An Irish language play (title is not currently known) by Eamonn O'Neill. Central Branch of the Gaelic League, Rotunda Hall, Dublin: 25 January 1905. (Scenery painted by Alice Milligan.)

16. Frank Fay poetry reading, O'Reilly's "Centenary Ode," Celtic Literary Society's celebration of the 124th anniversary of Robert Emmet's birth, Celtic Literary Society, Dublin: 4 March 1902.

17. *A Gallant of Galway* by James Duncan. National Literary Society, 6 St. Stephen's Green, Dublin: 24 March 1902. (Possibly presented two nights.)

18. *Deirdre* by AE (George Russell). Inghinidhe na hEireann, staged by Frank and William Fay, performed by W. G. Fay's Irish National Dramatic Society, St. Teresa's Total Abstinence Hall, Dublin: 2, 3, 4 April 1902.

19. *Kathleen Ni Houlihan* by W. B. Yeats. Same theatre, staging credits and location as above: 2, 3, 4 April 1902.

20. *Ar Son Baile Agus Tire (For the Sake of Home and Country)* by (?).

    O'Dorney. The Cleaver Branch of the Gaelic League, Rotunda Hall Dublin: 16, 17 May 1902.

21. *An Tincear Agus An tSidheog (The Tinker and the Sheeog)* by Douglas Hyde. Performed in the garden of George Moore, Eily Place, Dublin: 19 May 1902.

22. *Kitty* by Mary E. L. Butler. Performed by small theatre groups in Counties Sligo and Cork: Spring/Summer 1902. Specific dates and locations are not known.

23. *Ar Son Baile Agus Tire (For the Sake of Home and Country)* by O'Dorney. The Cleaver Branch of the Gaelic League, Rotunda Hall Dublin: 5 July 1902.

24. "A Dialogue in Irish by Two Members of the Irish National Dramatic Company." Irish National Theatre Society, Staged by Frank Fay, People's Park, Dunleary, 21 August 1902.

25. *An Posadh (The Marriage)* by Douglas Hyde. Performed at the 1902 Connacht Feis by a Gaelic League branch, Galway: August 1902.

26. *Hugh Roe O'Donnell* by Standish O'Grady. The Cave Hill Social Club of Belfast (the "Neophytes"), within woods of Sheestown, County Kilkenny: 15 August 1902.

27. *An Sprid (The Ghost)* by Father O'Leary. A Gaelic League Branch, Munster Feis: September 1902.

28. *Deirdre* by AE. The Irish National Theatre Society (formed by W.B. Yeats, AE and the Fays) Antient Concert, Rooms, Dublin: 28, 30 October 1902.

29. *Kathleen Ni Houlihan* by W. B. Yeats. Same theatre and location as above: 28 October and 1 November 1902.

30. *The Sleep of the King* by James Cousins. Same theatre and location as above: 29 October 1902.

31. *The Laying of the Foundations* by Frederick Ryan. Same theatre and location as above: 29, 31 October and 1 November 1902.

32. *Eilis agus an Bhean Deirce (Lizzie and the Beggarwoman)* by P.T. MacGinley. Same theatre and location as above: 29, 31 October 1902.

33. *The Pot of Broth* by W. B. Yeats. Same theatre and location as above: 30 October, 1 November 1902.

34. *The Racing Lug* by James Cousins. Same theatre and location as above: 31 October 1902.

35. *An Tobar Draoidheachta (The Magic Well)* by Father Dinneen. Keating Branch of the Gaelic League, Dublin: 14 November 1902.

36. *The Pot of Broth* by W. B. Yeats. The Irish National Theatre Society, Camden Street Hall Dublin: 4, 5, 6 December 1902.

37. *The Laying of the Foundations* by Frederick Ryan. Same theatre and location as above: 4, 5, 6 December 1902.

1903

38. *An Naomh ar Iarraid (The Lost Saint)* by Douglas Hyde. Inghinidhe na hEireann, performed by members of Inghinidhe na hEireann's children classes, Dublin Workman's Total Abstinence Association Hall, 41 York Street, Dublin: 19, 30 January 1903.

39. *An Posadh (The Marriage)* by Douglas Hyde. Ard Chraobh de Chonnradh na Gaedhilge (Central Branch of the Gaelic League), staged by Miss Curran of Inghinidhe na hEireann, Rotunda Hall Dublin: 12, 13, 14 February 1903.

40. *Aodh ONeill (Hugh ONeill)* by Conan Maol. Same theatre (organization) and location as above: 12, 13 and 14 February 1903.

41. *An Sprid (The Ghost)* by Father O'Leary. Same theatre and location as above: 12, 13 and 14 February 1903. (Occasionally this play was referred to by its bilingual title, *An Spirit,* as in September 1902.)

42. *An Naomh ar Iarraid (The Lost Saint)* by Douglas Hyde. Gaelic Athletic Association (G. A. A.) for their second annual convention, (possibly performed by the Inghinidhe na hEireann children's group) Dublin: 23 February 1903.

43. *An Tailliur Cleasach (The Trickster Tailor)* by P. T. MacGinley. Dramatic Class of Cumann Litiordha Colmchille: 7 March 1903.

44. A note in the 21 February 1903 *United Irishman* states that, according to AE, a man named Michael Waldron of Ballyhaunis, County Mayo, had written a number of plays which had been performed in parts of Mayo.

45. *Emmet and Napoleon,* "a dialogue in costume" by Henry Connell Mangan. The Irish National Theatre Society for the Cumann na nGaedheal Celtic Literary Society Branch's Emmet Centenary commemoration, Rotunda Hall, Dublin: 9 March 1903.

46. *The Hour Glass* by W. B. Yeats. The Irish National Theatre Society, Molesworth Hall, Molesworth Street, Dublin: 14 March 1903.

47. *Twenty-five* by Lady Gregory. Same theatre and location as above: 14 March 1903.

48. *An Tobar Draoidheachta (The Magic Well)* by Father Dineen. North Parish Gaelic League Branch, St. Mary's Hall, Cork: 17 March 1903.

49. *The Laying of the Foundations* by Frederick Ryan. The Irish National Theatre Society for (James Connolly's) Irish Socialist Republican Party's "Grand Concert and Dramatic Entertainment," Rotunda Hall, Dublin: 30 March 1903.

50. *The Sword of Dermot* by James Cousins. The National Literary Society (most likely performed by members of the Irish National Theatre Society), National Literary Society's Hall, Dublin: 20 April 1903.

51. *Airgeal Croise Caoile (The Narrow Silver Cross)* by (?). Performed by Maynooth College students, Maynooth: (?) April 1903.

52. *Aodh ONeill (Hugh ONeill)* by Conan Maol. Cumann Ceoil Drama, (most likely at the Rotunda Hall), Dublin: 28 April 1903.

53. *Tadhg Saor (Free Man)* by Father O'Leary. Keating Branch of the Gaelic League, Grocer's Assistants' Hall (sometimes referred to as the Banba Hall), Rutland Square (now Parnell Square), Dublin: 3 May 1903.

54. *An Mi-Adh Mor (The Great Ill-luck)* by W. P. Ryan. Inghinidhe na hEireann students for the Mangan Centenary Celebration, Rotunda Hall, Dublin: early May 1903.

55. *Pleusgadh na Bulgoide (The Bursting of the Bubble)* by Douglas Hyde. Same organization and location as above: early May 1903.

56. *The Saxon Shillin'* by Padraic Colum. Inghinidhe na hEireann students, Grocer's Assistants' Hall, Rutland Square, Dublin: 15, 16, 17 May 1903.

57. *An Naomh ar Iarraid (The Lost Saint)* by Douglas Hyde. Same organization and location as above: 15, 16, 17 May 1903.

58. *Dochtuireacht Nuadh (The New Doctoring)* by P. T. MacGinley. Same organization and location as above: 15, 16, 17 May 1903.

59. *Muirgheis* (an Irish opera) by Mr. O'Brien Butler and Nora Glesson (with George Moore). Same organization and location as above—Only the first act was performed: 16 May 1903.

60. *Deirdre* by AE. The Irish National Theatre Society, open-air performance, grounds of the Dun Emer Press, Dundrum, County Dublin: Spring 1903.

61. *The Pot of Broth* by W.B. Yeats. The Irish National Theatre Society, Town Hall in Loughrea, County Galway: Spring 1903.

62. *Deirdre* by AE. Same theatre and location as above: Spring 1903.

63. *Casadh an tSugain (The Twisting of the Rope)* by Douglas Hyde. A County Mayo (?) branch of the Gaelic League for the Feis Naoimh in Ballina, Mayo: June 1903.

64. *The Heather Field* by Edward Martyn. The Players' Club, Queen's Theatre, Dublin: June 1903.

65. *A Twinkle in Ireland's Eye* by Joseph Ryan. Celtic Literary Society, Workman's Hall, York Street, Dublin: 17, 18 July 1903.

66. *An Doctuir (The Doctor)* by Seumas O'Beirne. Tawin Players, Galway: 1 August 1903.

67. *Hugh ONeill* by Eamon ONeill. (Translated from *Aodh ONeill.*) Students of Mount Melleray, Dungarvan: August 1903.

68. An Irish language play (title is not currently known) by E. L. O'Toole. A County Galway (?) branch of the Gaelic League for the Feis Connacht in Galway: August 1903.

69. *An Cleamhnas (The Matchmaking)* by Douglas Hyde. Same organization and location as above: August 1903.

70. *The King's Threshold* by W. B. Yeats. The Irish National Theatre Society, Molesworth Hall Dublin: 8, 9, 10 October 1903.

71. *In the Shadow of the Glen* by John Synge. Same theatre and location as above: 8, 9, 10 October 1903.

72. *Kathleen Ni Houlihan* by W. B. Yeats. Same theatre and location as above: 8, 9 and 10 October 1903.

73. *Kathleen Ni Houlihan* by W. B. Yeats. The Ulster Literary Theatre (with Dudley Digges and Maire Quinn of the Cumann na nGaedhael Irish Theatre Company, formerly actors of the Irish National Theatre Society), St. Mary's Hall, Belfast: mid October 1903.

74. *The Racing Lug* by James Cousins. Same theatre and location as above: mid October 1903.

75. *Tadhg Saor (Free Man)* by Father O'Leary. Keating Branch of the Gaelic League, Rotunda Hall, Dublin: 17 October 1903.

76. *Kathleen Ni Houlihan* by W. B. Yeats. Cumann na nGaedhael Irish Theatre Company, Molesworth Hall, Dublin: 31 October 1903. (Sometimes this theatre was known as the Cumann na Aisteoiri Naisiunta or National Players Society.)

77. *Robert Emmet* by Henry Connell (Henry Connell Mangan). Same theatre and location as above: 31 October and 4 November 1903.

78. *Pleusgadh na Bulgoide (The Bursting of the Bubble)* by Douglas Hyde. Same theatre and location as above: 2, 4 November 1903.

79. *The Sword of Dermot* by James Cousins. Same theatre and location as above: 2 November 1903.

80. *A Man's Foes* by James Cousins. Same theatre and location as above: 3 November 1903.

81. *A Twinkle in Ireland's Eye* by Joseph Ryan. Same theatre and location as above: 3 November 1903.

82. *An Doctuir (The Doctor)* by Seumas O'Beirne. Tawin Players, Banba Hall, Dublin: 13 November 1903.

83. *The Hour Glass* by W. B. Yeats. The Irish National Theatre Society, Molesworth Hall, Dublin: 3, 4, 5 December 1903.

84. *Broken Soil* by Padraic Colum. Same theatre and location as above: 3, 4, 5 December 1903.

85. *A Pot of Broth* by W. B. Yeats. Same theatre and location as above: 3, 4, 5 December 1903.

86. *Muirgheis* (an Irish Opera) by Mr. O'Brien Butler and Nora Glesson (with George Moore). Keating Branch of the Gaelic League, Theatre Royal, Dublin: 7 December 1903.

1904

87. *The Shadowy Waters* by W. B. Yeats. The Irish National Theatre Society, Molesworth Hall, Dublin: 14, 15, 16 January 1904.

88. *Twenty-five* by Lady Gregory. Same theatre and location as above: 14, 15, 16 January 1904.

89. *The Townland of Tamney* by Seumas MacManus. Same theatre location as above: 14, 15, 16 January 1904.

90. *Robert Emmet* by Henry Connell Mangan. Cumann na nGaedhael Irish Theatre Company, Rathmines Town Hall: 30 January and 1 February 1904.

91. *An Posadh (The Marriage)* by Douglas Hyde. Same theatre and location as above: 30 January and 1 February 1904.

92. *A Man's Foes* by James Cousins. Same theatre and location as above: 30 January and 1 February 1904.

93. *Deirdre* by AE. The Irish National Theatre Society, Molesworth Hall, Dublin: 25, 26, 27 February 1904.

94. *Riders to the Sea* by John Synge. Same theatre and location as above: 25, 26, 27 February 1904.

95. *An Posadh (The Marriage)* by Douglas Hyde. Cumann na nGaedhael Irish Players Society (also referred to as the National Players Society), Banba Hall, Dublin: 21 March 1904.

96. *An Enchanted Sea* by Edward Martyn. The Players' Club, Antient Concert Rooms, Dublin: 18, 19 April 1904.

97. *Tenement Troubles* by Susan Varian. Performed by (?), for the All-Ireland Temperance Bazaar, Dublin: (?) May 1904.

98. *An Dochtuir (The Doctor)* by Seumas O'Beirne. Tawin Players, for the Feis in Athlone: early July 1904.

99. *An Posadh (The Marriage)* by Douglas Hyde. Ballina Dramatic Club, Knockmore, County Mayo: early July, 1904.

100. *The Hard-Hearted Man* by Seumas MacManus. Catholic Boys' Brigade, Richmond Hill, Rathmines, County Dublin: 10 July 1904.

101. *Seaghan na Scuab (The Tale of the Broom)* by Tomas O nAoda (Thomas Hays). A Gaelic League Branch (perhaps the Keating Branch), for the 1904 Oireachtas, Rotunda Hall, Dublin: 1, 6 August 1904.

102. *An Dochtuir (The Doctor)* by Seumas O'Beirne. Tawin Players, same location as above: 1, 6 August 1904.

103. *Hugh ONeill* by Eamon ONeill. Ursuline Convent Students, Cork: October 1904.

104. *The Deliverance of Red Hugh* by Alice Milligan. The National Players Society, Molesworth Hall, Dublin: 28 October and 1 November 1904.

105. *The Resurrection of Dinny O'Dowd* by Seumas MacManus. Same theatre and location as above: 31 October 1904.

106. *Seaghan na Scuab (The Tale of the Broom)* by Tomas O nAoda. Scheduled by the same theatre for the same location as above—but due to an illness of its author, who acted in the play, it was canceled. It had been scheduled for 28 October 1904.

107. *The Hard-Hearted Man* by Seumas MacManus. Same theatre and location as above: 29 October 1904.

108. *The International Exhibition* by Joseph Ryan. Same theatre and location as above: 29 October and 1 November 1904.

109. *The Magic Sieve* by John Hamilton. Same theatre and location as above: 31 October 1904.

110. *Casadh an tSugain (The Twisting of the Rope)* by Douglas Hyde. Keating Branch of the Gaelic League, Rotunda Hall, Dublin: 5 November 1904.

111. *The Last Irish King* by T. ONeill Russell. Cork National Theatre, Clarence Hall, the Imperial Hotel Cork: 9 (and maybe 10) December 1904.

112. *A Pot of Broth* by W. B. Yeats. Same theatre and location as above: 9 (and maybe 10) December 1904.

113. *The Resurrection of Dinny O'Dowd* by Seumas MacManus. National Players Society, Banba Hall: 10 December 1904.

114. *Brian of Banba* by Bulmer Hobson. The Ulster Literary Theatre, Ulster Minor Hall, Belfast: 7, 8 (as well as two additional nights the following week) December 1904.

115. *The Reformers* by Lewis Purcell (Davis Parkhill). Same theatre and location as above: 7, 8 (as well as two additional nights the following week) December 1904.

116. *On Baile's Strand* by W. B. Yeats. The Irish National Theatre Society, Abbey Theatre, Dublin: 27, 28, 29, 30, 31 December 1904 and 2, 3 January 1905. (This production, with its accompanying productions, opened the Abbey Theatre.)

117. *Spreading the News* by Lady Gregory. Same theatre and location as above: 27, 28, 29, 30, 31 December 1904 and 2, 3 January 1905.

118. *Kathleen Ni Houlihan* by W. B. Yeats. Same theatre and location as above: 27, 29, 31 December 1904.

119. *In the Shadow of the Glen* by John Synge. Same theatre and location as above: 28, 30 December 1904 and 2, 3 January 1905.

120. *Drama Breith Criosta (The Nativity)* by Douglas Hyde. This was scheduled for production in County Kilkenny during December, but was canceled due to a ban imposed by Catholic clergy.

1905

121. *Teach na nBocht (The Poorhouse)* by Douglas Hyde. The National Players Society, Gaelic League Hall, Rathmines Road, Dublin: 21, 22 January 1905.

122. *The Resurrection of Dinny O'Dowd* by Seumas MacManus. Same theatre and location as above: 21, 22 January 1905.

123. *The Hard-Hearted Man* by Seumas MacManus. The National Players Society, Town Hall Dalkey: 30 January 1905.

124. *The Resurrection of Dinny O'Dowd* by Seumas MacManus. Same theatre and location as above: 30 January 1905.

125. *The Well of Saints* by John Synge. The Irish National Theatre Society, Abbey Theatre, Dublin: 4, 6, 7, 8, 9, 10, 11 February 1905.

126. *The Lad from Largymore* by Seumas MacManus. The National Players Society, Rotunda Hall, Dublin: 27 February 1905.

127. *The Last of the Desmonds* by Alice Milligan. The Cork National Theatre, Assembly Rooms, Cork: 6 (and possibly 7, 8) March 1905.

128. *Kathleen Ni Houlihan* by W. B. Yeats. Same theatre and location as above: 6 (and possibly 7, 8) March 1905.

129. *The Nation Builders* by John O'Loughlin. Same theatre and location as above: 6 (and possibly 7, 8) March 1905.

130. *Pleusgadh na Bulgoide (The Bursting of the Bubble)* by Douglas Hyde. The National Players Society, Queen's Theatre, Dublin: 17 March 1905. (Like the Gaiety Theatre, the Queens was occasionally, but rarely, rented by Theatre Movement factions.)

131. *The Lad from Largymore* by Seumas MacManus. Same theatre and location as above: 17 March 1905.

132. *The Resurrection of Dinny O'Dowd* by Seumas MacManus. Same theatre and location as above: 17 March 1905.

133. *Robert Emmet* by Henry Connell Mangan. Theatre unknown, Derry: 17 March 1905.

134. *Kincora* by Lady Gregory. The Irish National Theatre Society, Abbey Theatre, Dublin: 25, 26, 27, 28 (and possibly 29, 30 and 1 April) March 1905.

135. *Kincora* by Lady Gregory. The Irish National Theatre Society, Abbey Theatre, Dublin: 24 April (and alternating during the week with the following production) 1905.

136. *The Building Fund* by William Boyle. Same theatre and location as above: 25 April (and alternating during the week with above production) 1905.

137. *The Little Cowherd of Slainge* by Joseph Campbell. The Ulster Literary Theatre, the Clarence Place Hall, Belfast: 4, 5, 6 May 1905.

138. *The Enthusiast* by Lewis Purcell (David Parkhill). Same theatre and location as above: 4, 5, 6 May 1905.

139. *The Trail of the Serpent* by Thomas Markham. Theatre unknown, Banba Hall, Dublin: 28 May 1905.

140. *The Hour Glass* by W. B. Yeats. The Irish National Theatre Society, Abbey Theatre, Dublin: 9, 10, 12, 13, 14, 15, 16, 17 June 1905.

141. *The Land* by Padraic Colum Same theatre and location as above: 9, 10, 12, 13, 14, 15, 16, 17 June 1905.

142. *An Tincear agus an tSidheog (.The Tinker and the Sheeog)* by Douglas Hyde. A Gaelic League Branch (possibly the Keating Branch), for the Oireachtas, Rotunda Hall, Dublin: 14, 19 August 1905.

143. *Caitlin Ni hCallachain* (translation of Yeats' *Kathleen Ni Houlihan*) by Father O'Kelly. Same theatre and location, for the Oireachtas: 14 August 1905.

144. An Irish language play (title is not currently known) by (?). The Galway Branch of the Gaelic League, for the Oireachtas, Rotunda Hall, Dublin: 19 August 1905.

145. Newspaper notes indicate that Irish dramas were performed by the National Players Society for the MacMurrough Branch Workingmen's Club in Inchicore: 27 August 1905. The specific plays are not known.

146. *Seaghan na Scuab (The Tale of the Broom)* by Tomas O hAodha. The Keating Branch of the Gaelic League, Abbey Theatre, Dublin: 27 October 1905. (The Irish National Theatre Society [later the National Theatre Society] sometimes rented the Abbey stage to other theatre groups.)

147. *Creideamh agus Gorta (Faith and Famine)* by Father Dineen. Same theatre and location as above: 28 October 1905.

148. *An Posadh (The Marriage)* by Douglas Hyde. The National Players Society, Molesworth Hall, Dublin: 30 October, 1 November 1905.

149. *Boycotting* by Lady Gilbert and Rosa Mulholland. Same theatre and location as above: 31 October and 3 November 1905.

150. *The Lad from Largymore* by Seumas MacManus. Same theatre and location as above: 31 October and 3 November 1905.

151. *Teach na nBocht (The Poorhouse)* by Douglas Hyde. Same theatre and location as above: 31 October and 2, 4 November 1905.

152. *The Tale of the Town* by Edward Martyn. Same theatre and location as above: 31 October and 2, 4 November 1905.

153. *The Woman of the Seven Sorrows* by Seumas MacManus. Same theatre and location as above: 1, 3 November 1905.

154. *The Leadin' Road to Donegal* by Seumas MacManus. Same theatre and location as above: 1 November 1905.

155. *The Leadin' Road to Donegal* by Seumas MacManus. The Mount Argus Branch of the Gaelic League (even though a play in English), St. Kevin's Hall, (?) 4 December 1905.

156. *The Saxon Schillin'* by Padraic Colum. Performed by members of the National Players Society, Banba Hall, Dublin: 16 December 1905.

157. *The White Cockade* by Lady Gregory. The National Theatre Society Ltd. (formerly the Irish National Theatre Society), Abbey Theatre, Dublin: 9, 10, 11, 12, 13, 14, 15, 16 December 1905.

158. *Boycotting* by Lady Gilbert and Rosa Mulholland. The National Players Society, Molesworth Hall, Dublin: 26 December 1905.

159. *Tadg Saor (Free Man)* by Father O'Leary. Same theatre and location as above: 26 December 1905.

160. *Leadin' the Road to Donegal* by Seumas MacManus. Same theatre and location as above: 26 December 1905.

161. *The Resurrection of Dinny O'Dowd* by Seumas MacManus. Same theatre and location as above: 26 December 1905.

162. *The Saxon Schillin'* by Padraic Colum. Same theatre and location as above: 26 December, 1905.

163. *The Hard-Hearted Man* by Seumas MacManus. Same theatre and location as above: 27 December 1905.

164. *The Lad from Largymore* by Seumas MacManus. Same theatre and location as above: 27 December 1905.

165. *Sold* by James Cousins. The Cork National Theatre, hall/theatre is unknown, Cork: 27 (possibly more dates) December 1905. (There was probably another play on the bill.)

1906

166. *Riders to the Sea* by John Synge. The National Theatre Society Ltd., Abbey Theatre, Dublin: 20, 22, 23, 24, 25, 26, 27 January 1906.

167. *The Eloquent Dempsey* by William Boyle. Same theatre and location as above: 20, 22, 23, 24, 25, 26, 27 January 1906.

168. *An Tincear agus tSidheog (The Tinker and the Sheeog)* by Douglas Hyde. The Limerick Branch of the Gaelic League, Limerick Theatre, Limerick: mid January 1906.

169. *The Hard-Hearted Man* by Seumas MacManus. Same theatre and location as above (even though a play in English): mid January 1906.

170. *The Hour Glass* by W. B. Yeats. The National Theatre Society Ltd., Abbey Theatre, Dublin: 19, 20, 23, 24 February 1906.

171. *Hyacinth Halvey* by Lady Gregory. Same theatre and location as above: 19, 20, 23, 24 February 1906.

172. *Kathleen Ni Houlihan* by W. B. Yeats. Same theatre and location as above: 19, 20, 23, 24 February 1906

173. *Riders to the Sea* by John Synge. Same theatre and location as above: 21, 22 February 1906.

174. *The Eloquent Dempsey* by William Boyle. Same theatre and location as above: 21, 22 February 1906.

175. *Galloping O'Hogan* by P. Ua Muineachain. Theatre unknown, Banba Hall, Dublin: 26 February 1906.

176. A brief tour of Ireland's smaller cities by the National Theatre Society Ltd. in March 1906: specifically at the Town Hall, Wexford on 10 March. The specific productions are not presently known.

177. *The Lad from Largymore* by Seumas MacManus. The National Players (formerly the National Players Society), Queen's Theater, Dublin: 17 March 1906.

178. *The Hard-Hearted Man* by Seumas MacManus. Same theatre and location as above: 17 March 1906.

179. *The White Horse of the Peppers* adapted from Samuel Lover's play with the degrading Irish charicatures supposedly removed. Playwright unknown. Same theatre and location as above: 17 March 1906.

180. *Red Hugh* by T. O'Neill Russell. Students of St. Patrick's College in Carlow, Carlow: 17 March 1906.

181. *Red Hugh* by T. O'Neill Russell. Pioneer Dramatic Society, St. Francis Xavier's Halt Dublin: 5 April 1906.

182. *On Baile's Strand* by W. B. Yeats. The National Theatre Society Ltd., Abbey Theatre, Dublin: 16, 18, 20, 21 April 1906.

183. *The Doctor in Spite of Himself* by Moliere, translated by Lady Gregory. Same theatre and location as above: 16, 18, 20, 21 April 1906.

184. *In the Shadow of the Glen* by John Synge. Same theatre and location as above: 16, 18, 20, 21 April 1906.

185. *The Building Fund* by William Boyle. Same theatre and location as above: 17, 19 April 1906.

186. *Spreading the News* by Lady Gregory. Same theatre location as above: 17, 19 April 1906.

187. *Rosaleen Dhu* by John Dever. Draper's Dramatic Society, Rotunda Hall, Dublin, 4, 5 May 1906.

188. *The Resurrection of Dinny O'Dowd* by Seumas MacManus. The National Players, Town Hall, Clontarf: 7 May 1906.

189. *The Last Feast of the Fianna* by Alice Milligan. Branch of the Five Provinces (including actors who seceded from the Abbey Theatre in December 1905), Hall unknown, Dublin (?) early (possibly 2) June 1906.

190. *Seabac na Ceathramha Caoile (The Hawk of Carrowkeel) by* Tomar O hAoda. Organization unknown, but probably a Gaelic League branch for the 1906 Oireachtas, Rotunda Hall, Dublin: 8, 11 August 1906.

191. *An tAthrughadh Mor (The Big Change)* (a bilingual play) by Felix Partridge. The Western Players for the 1906 Oireachtas, Rotunda Hall, Dublin: 9 August 1906.

192. *An Talinf* translated from Padraic Colum's *The Land* by Tohma. Performed by members of the newly formed Cluithcheoiri na hEireann (the Theatre of Ireland) for the 1906 Oireachtas, Rotunda Hall, Dublin: 9 August 1906.

193. *The Sword of Dermot* by James Cousins. The National Players Society, open-air performance, (?) Co. Dublin: 23 September 1906.

194. *The Gaol Gate* by Lady Gregory. The National Theatre Society Ltd., Abbey Theatre, Dublin: 20, 22, 23, 24, 25, 26, 27 October 1906.

195. *The Mineral Workers* by William Boyle. Same theatre and location as above: 20, 22, 23, 24, 25, 26, 27 October 1906.

196. *Spreading the News* by Lady Gregory. Same theatre and location as above: 20, 22, 23, 24, 25, 26, 27 October 1906.

197. *An tAthrughadh Mor (The Big Change)* by Felix Partridge. The National Players, Abbey Theatre, Dublin: 2, 5 November 1906.

198. *The Eloquent Dempsey* by William Boyle. The National Theatre Society Ltd., Abbey Theatre, Dublin: 17 November 1906.

199. *Kathleen Ni Houlihan* by W. B. Yeats. Same theatre and location as above: 17 November 1906.

200. *Deirdre* by W. B. Yeats. Same theatre and location as above: 24, 26, 27, 28, 29 30 November and 1, 3, 4, 5, 6, 7, 8 December 1906.

201. *The Canavans* by Lady Gregory. Same theatre and location as above: 24, 26, 27, 28, 29, 30 November 1906.

202. *The Building Fund* by William Boyle. Same theatre and location as above: 1, 3, 4, 5, 6, 7, 8 December 1906.

203. *Casadh an tSugain (The Twisting of the Rope)* by Douglas Hyde. Cluithcheoiri na hEireann (the Theatre of Ireland), Molesworth Hall, Dublin: 7, 8 December 1906.

204. *The Racing Lug* by James Cousins. Same theatre and location as above: 7, 8 December 1906.

205. *The Shadowy Waters* by W. B. Yeats. The National Theatre Society Ltd., Abbey Theatre, Dublin: 8, 10, 11, 12, 13, 14, 15 December 1906.

206. *The Canavans* by Lady Gregory. Same theatre and location as above: 8, 10, 11, 12, 13, 14, 15 December 1906.

207. *The Bailiff of Kilmore* by Joseph Ford. Possibly performed by the newly formed Sinn Fein Dramatic Society, Banba Hall, Dublin: 15 December 1906.

208. *The Turn of the Road* by Rutherford Mayne. The Ulster Literary Theatre, Ulster Minor Hall, Belfast: 17, 18, 19 December 1906.

209. *The Pagan* by Lewis Purcell. Same theatre and location as above: 17, 18, 19 December 1906.

210. *The White Horse of the Peppers* adapted from Samuel Lover's play, by (?). The National Players, Molesworth Hall, Dublin: 26, 27 December 1906.

211. *The Deliverance of Red Hugh* by Alice Milligan. Same theatre and location as above: 26 December 1906.

212. *An tAthrughadh Mor (The Big Change)* by Felix Partridge. Same theatre and location as above: 27 December 1906.

213. *The Hour Glass* by W. B. Yeats. The National Theatre Society Ltd., Abbey Theatre, Dublin: 29, 31 December 1906.

214. *The Mineral Workers* by William Boyle. Same theatre and location as above: 29, 31 December 1906.

1907

215. *The Hour Glass* by W. B. Yeats. The National Theatre Society Ltd., Abbey Theatre, Dublin: 1, 2, 3, 4, 6 January 1907.

216. *The Mineral Workers* by William Boyle. Same theatre and location as above: 1, 2, 3, 4, 5, 6 January 1907.

217. *Riders to the Sea* by John Synge. The National Theatre Society Ltd., Abbey Theatre, Dublin: 12 January 1907.

218. *The Eloquent Dempsey* by William Boyle. Same theatre and location as above: 12 January 1907.

219. *Hyacinth Halvey* by Lady Gregory. Same theatre and location as above: 19 January 1907.

220. *In the Shadow of the Glen* by John Synge. Same theatre and location as above: 19 January 1907.

221. *Spreading the News* by Lady Gregory. Same theatre and location as above: 19 January 1907.

222. *Kathleen Ni Houlihan* by W. B. Yeats. Same theatre and location as above: 19 January 1907.

223. *The Playboy of the Western World* by John Synge. Same theatre and location as above: 26, 28, 29, 30, 31 January and 1, 2 February 1907.

224. *Riders to the Sea* by John Synge. Same theatre and location as above: 26, 28, 29, 30, 31 January and 1, 2 February 1907.

On Monday evening, 4 February 1907, the National Theatre Society Ltd. held a public debate on John Synge's *The Playboy of the Western World* in the Abbey Theatre. While not a theatre production, admission was charged.

225. *A West-Briton's Romance* by (?). The Boothe Branch of the Gaelic League, County Hall Boothe: 4, 5 February 1907.

226. *Rosaleen Dhu* by John Dever. The Draper's Dramatic Society, Rotunda Hall, Dublin: 4, 5, 6, 7, 8, 9 February 1907.

227. *The Fiddler's House* by Padraic Colum. The Cluithcheoiri na hEireann (the Theatre of Ireland), Abbey Theatre, Dublin: 11, 12 February 1907.

228. *The Last Feast of the Fianna* by Alice Milligan. Same theatre and location as the above: 11, 12 February 1907.

229. *The Pot of Broth* by W. B. Yeats. The National Theatre Society Ltd., Abbey Theatre, Dublin: 9 February 1907.

230. *The Doctor in Spite of Himself* by Moliere, translated by Lady Gregory. Same theatre as above: 9 February 1907.

231. *Kathleen Ni Houlihan* by W. B. Yeats. Same theatre and location as above: 9 February 1907.

232. *The White Cockade* by Lady Gregory. Same theatre and location as above: 23, 25, 26, 27, 28 February and 1, 2 March 1907.

233. *The Jackdaw* by Lady Gregory. Same theatre and location as above: 23, 25, 26, 27, 28 February and 1, 2 March 1907.

234. *The Rising of the Moon* by Lady Gregory. Same theatre and location as above: 9 March 1907.

235. *The Hour Glass* by W. B. Yeats. Same theatre and location as above: 9 March 1907.

236. *The Gaol Gate* by Lady Gregory. Same theatre and location as above: 9 March 1907.

237. *Hyacinth Halvey* by Lady Gregory. Same theatre and location as above: 9 March 1907.

238. *On Baile's Strand* by W. B. Yeats. Same theatre and location as above: 16 March 1907.

239. *Interior* by Maurice Maeterlinck. Same theatre and location as above: 16 March 1907.

Such continental plays were produced by the Irish Theatre Movement in an effort to nationalistically promote Dublin as a leading cultural European city.

240. *Kathleen Ni Houlihan* by W. B. Yeats. Same theatre and location as above: 16 March 1907.

241. *The Rapparee* by Gerald O'Loughlin. The National Players, Queen's Theatre: 17 March 1907.

242. *Sold* by James Cousins. Same theatre and location as above: 17 March 1907.

243. *An tAthrughadh Mor (The Big Change)* by Felix Partridge. Same theatre and location as above: 17 March 1907.

244. *The Fiddler's House* by Padraic Colum The Cluithcheoiri na hEireann (the Theatre of Ireland), Rotunda Hall, Dublin: 21, 22, 23 March 1907.

245. *The Last Feast of the Fianna* by Alice Milligan. Same theatre and location as above: 21, 22, 23 March 1907.

246. *The Doctor in Spite of Himself* by Moliere, translated by Lady Gregory. The National Theatre Society Ltd., Abbey Theatre, Dublin: 23 March 1907.

247. *Interior* by Maurice Maeterlinck. Same theatre and location as above: 23 March 1907.

248. *The Rising of the Moon* by Lady Gregory. Same theatre and location as above: 23 March 1907.

249. *Spreading the News* by Lady Gregory. Same theatre and location as above: 23 March 1907.

250. *The Pagan* by Lewis Purcell (David Parkhill). The Ulster Literary Theatre, Abbey Theatre, Dublin: 30 March 1907.

251. *The Turn of the Road* by Rutherford Mayne. Same theatre and location as above: 30 March 1907.

252. *The Eyes of the Blind* by Winified M. Letts. The National Theatre Society Ltd., Abbey Theatre, Dublin: 1, 2, 3, 4, 5, 6 April 1907.

This and the following productions which shared the same performance dates, alternated between evening and matinee slots for Easter Week.

253. *The Poorhouse* (later re-titled *The Workhouse Ward*) by Lady Gregory and Douglas Hyde. Same theatre and location as above: 1, 2, 3, 4, 5, 6 April 1907.

254. *The Rising of the Moon* by Lady Gregory. Same theatre and location as above: 1, 2, 3, 4, 5, 6 April 1907.

255. *The Jackdaw* by Lady Gregory. Same theatre and location as above: 1, 2, 3, 4, 5, 6 April 1907.

256. *Spreading the News* by Lady Gregory. Same theatre and location as above: 1, 2, 3, 4, 5, 6 April 1907.

257. *Hyacinth Halvey* by Lady Gregory. Same theatre and location as above: 1, 2, 3, 4, 5, 6 April 1907.

258. *The Gaol Gate* by Lady Gregory. Same theatre and location as above: 1, 2, 3, 4, 5, 6 April 1907.

259. *Riders to the Sea* by John Synge. Same theatre and location as above: 1, 2, 3, 4, 5, 6 April 1907.

260. *Deirdre* by W. B. Yeats. Same theatre and location as above: 1, 2, 3, 4, 5, 6 April 1907.

261. *Kathleen Ni Houlihan* by W. B. Yeats. Same theatre and location as above: 1, 2, 3, 4, 5, 6 April 1907.

262. *Robert Emmet* by Henry Connell Mangan. The Sinn Fein Dramatic Society, Molesworth Hall, Dublin: 8, 9 April 1907.

263. *An tAthrughadh Mor (The Big Change)* by Felix Partridge. The Keating Branch of the Gaelic League, Rotunda Hall, Dublin: 24 April 1907.

264. *The Eyes of the Blind* by Winifed M. Letts. The National Theatre Society Ltd., Abbey Theatre, Dublin: 27 April 1907.

265. *Fand* by Wilfred Scawen Blunt. Same theatre and location as above: 27 April 1907.

266. *A Pot of Broth* by W. B. Yeats. Same theatre and location as above: 27 April 1907.

267. *Kathleen Ni Houlihan* by W. B. Yeats. The National Theatre Society Ltd., Cork Opera House, Cork: 15, 16, 17 August 1907.

It is not presently known what other plays were on the bill with the above production.

268. "Irish Plays" were presented by the National Theatre Society Ltd., Abbey Theatre, Dublin: 26, 27, 28, 29, 30, 31 August 1907. The specific titles are not available.

269. *The Country Dressmaker* by George Fitzmaurice. The National Theatre Society Ltd., Abbey Theatre, Dublin: 3, 4, 5, 12, 13, 14 October 1907.

270. *In the Shadow of the Glen* by John Synge. Same theatre and location as above: 17, 18, 19 October 1907.

271. *The Land* by Padraic Colum. Same theatre and location as above: 17, 18, 19 October 1907.

272. *The Rising of the Moon* by Lady Gregory. Same theatre and location as above: 17, 18, 19 October 1907.

273. *O'Donnell's Cross* by Miss L. MacManus. Organization unknown, Rotunda Hall, Dublin: 2 November 1907.

274. *Before Clonmel* by R. G. Walsh. Same organization and location as above: 2 November 1907.

275. *Derrorgilla* by Lady Gregory. The National Theatre Society Ltd., Abbey Theatre, Dublin: 31 October and 1, 2, November 1907.

276. *The Canavans* by Lady Gregory. Same theatre and location as above: 31 October and 1, 2, November 1907.

277. *Hyacinth Halvey* by Lady Gregory. Same theatre and location as above: 7, 8, 9 November 1907.

278. *The Hour Glass* by W. B. Yeats. Same theatre and location as above: 7, 8, 9 November 1907.

279. *The Land* by Padraic Colum. Same theatre and location as above: 7, 8, 9 November 1907.

280. *Dervorgilla* by Lady Gregory. Same theatre and location as above: 14, 15, 16 November 1907.

281. *The Canavans* by Lady Gregory. Same theatre and location as above: 14, 15, 16 November 1907.

282. *The Unicorn form the Stars* by W. B. Yeats and Lady Gregory. Same theatre and location as above: 21, 22, 23 November 1907.

283. *Spreading the News* by Lady Gregory. Same theatre and location as above: 21, 22, 23 November 1907.

284. *Deirdre* by AE. The Cluithcheoiri na hEireann (the Theatre of Ireland), Abbey Theatre, Dublin: 13, 14 December 1907.

285. *The Matchmakers* by Seumas O'Kelly. Same theatre and location as above: 13, 14 December 1907.

286. *Suzanne and the Sovereigns* by Lewis Purcell (David Parkhill) and Gerald MacNamara. The Ulster Literary Theatre, Exhibition Hall, Belfast: 26–(?) December 1907.

This production may have shared the bill with other plays.

1908

287. *The Man Who Missed the Tide* by W. F. Casey. The National Theatre Society Ltd., Abbey Theatre, Dublin: 13, 14, 15 February 1908.

288. *The Piper* by Norreys Connell (Conal O'Riordan). Same theatre and location as above: 13, 14, 15 February 1908.

289. *The Gaol Gate* by Lady Gregory. The National Theatre Society Ltd., Abbey Theatre, Dublin: 7 March 1908.

290. *In the Shadow of the Glen* by John Synge. Same theatre and location as above: 7 March 1908.

291. *The Hour Glass* by W. B. Yeats. Same theatre and location as above: 7 March 1908.

292. *The Rising of the Moon* by Lady Gregory. Same theatre and location as above: 7 March 1908.

293. *Seymour's Redemption* by Count Casimir de Markievicz. The Independent Dramatic Company, Abbey Theatre, Dublin: 9 March 1908.

This is not necessarily an Irish production, but is listed here as part of the Irish Theatre Movement because the Independent Dramatic Co. of Casimir and Constance de Markievicz eventually did produce plays that clearly belonged to the Movement. This was their first offering.

294. "Irish Plays" were presented by the National Theatre Society Ltd., Abbey Theatre, Dublin: 17 March 1908. The specific titles are not available.

295. *Tega* by H. Sudermann, translated by Lady Gregory. The National Theatre Society Ltd., Abbey Theatre, Dublin: 19, 20, 21 March 1908.

296. *The Pie-dish* by George Fitzmaurice. Same theatre and location as above: 19, 20, 21 March 1908.

297. *The Golden Helmet* by W. B. Yeats. Same theatre and location as above: 19, 20, 21 March 1908.

298. *Hyacinth Halvey* by Lady Gregory. Same theatre and location as above: 4, 9, 10, 11, 20 April 1908.

299. *The Roguries of Scapin* by Moliere, translated by Lady Gregory. Same theatre and location as above: 4, 9, 10, 11 April 1908.

300. *In the Shadow of the Glen* by John Synge. Same theatre and location as above: 20 April 1908.

301. *The Rising of the Moon* by Lady Gregory. Same theatre and location as above: 20 April 1908.

302. *The Workhouse Ward* by Lady Gregory and Douglas Hyde. Same theatre and location as above: 20, 30 April 1908.

303. *The Drone* by Rutherford Mayne. The Ulster Literary Theatre, Abbey Theatre, Dublin: 24, 25 April 1908.

304. *Leaders of the People* by Robert Harding. Same theatre and location as above: 24, 25 April 1908.

305. *The Workhouse Ward* by Lady Gregory and Douglas Hyde. The National Theatre Society Ltd., Abbey Theatre, Dublin: 30 April and 1, 2 May 1908.

306. *The Man Who Missed the Tide* by W. F. Casey. Same theatre and location as above: 30 April and 1, 2 May 1908.

307. *The Doctor in Spite of Himself* by Moliere, translated by Lady Gregory. Same theatre and location as above: 9, 14, 15, 16 May 1908.

308. *Riders to the Sea* by John Synge. Same theatre and location as above: 9 May 1908.

309. *Spreading the News* by Lady Gregory. Same theatre and location as above: 9 May 1908.

310. *The Well of Saints* by John Synge. Same theatre and location as above: 14, 15, 16 May 1908.

311. *The Miracle of the Corn* by Padraic Colum. Cluithcheoiri na hEireann (Theatre of Ireland), Abbey Theatre, Dublin: 22, 23 May 1908.

312. *Maeve* by Edward Martyn. Same theatre and location as above: 22, 23 May 1908.

313. *The Enthusiast* by Lewis Purcell. Same theatre and location as above: 22, 23 May 1908.

314. *The Scheming Lieutenant* by Richard Brinsley Sheridan. The National Theatre Society Ltd., Abbey Theater, Dublin: 29, 30 May 1908.

315. *The Workhouse Ward* by Lady Gregory and Douglas Hyde. Same theatre and location as above: 29, 30 May 1908.

316. *Dervorgilla* by Lady Gregory. Same theatre and location as above: 29, 30 May 1908.

317. *The Jackdaw* by Lady Gregory. Same theatre and location as above: 29, 30 May 1908.

318. *Fate of the Children of Tuireann,* "an Irish pageant," staged by Fred Morrow, Cluithcheoiri na hEireann (Theatre of Ireland), on the grounds of St. Ann's, Donnybrook: summer 1908.

319. *Bairbre Ruadh* by Padraig O Conaire. A Gaelic League Branch for the 1908 Oireachtas, Rotunda Hall, Dublin: 6 August 1908. ("Bairbre Ruadh" is a Gaelic name.)

320. *Ar Thaoibh an Locha (The Side of the Lake)* by An Tatair O Ceallaig. Same theatre and location as above: 6 August 1908.

321. *Mac Carthaigh Mor (The Big Macartan)* by Padraig O Seagda. Same theatre and location as above: 7 August 1908.

322. An Irish language play (title is not currently known) by Maire ni Cinneide. Same theatre and location as above: 7 August 1908.

323. *The Rising of the Moon* by Lady Gregory. The National Theatre Society Ltd., Abbey Theatre, Dublin: 24, 25, 26, 27, 28, 29 August 1908.

324. *Kathleen Ni Houlihan* by W. B. Yeats. Same theatre and location as above: 24, 25, 26, 27, 28, 29 August 1908.

325. *The Rogueries of Scapin* by Moliere, translated by Lady Gregory. Same theatre and location as above: 24, 25, 26, 27, 28, 29 August 1908.

326. *The Man Who Missed the Tide* by W. F. Casey. Same theatre and location as above: 24, 25, 26, 27, 28, 29 August 1908.

327. *The Gaol Gate* by Lady Gregory. Same theatre and location as above: 24, 25, 26, 27, 28, 29 August 1908.

328. *The Jackdaw* by Lady Gregory. Same theatre and location as above: 24, 25, 26, 27, 28, 29 August 1908.

329. *The Rising of the Moon* by Lady Gregory. Same theatre and location as above: 3, 4, 5, 7, 9 September 1908.

330. *The Golden Helmet* by W. B. Yeats. Same theatre and location as above: 3, 4, 5, 7, 9 September 1908.

331. *Kathleen Ni Houlihan* by W. B. Yeats. Same theatre and location as above: 3, 4, 5, 7, 9 September 1908.

332. *Spreading the News* by Lady Gregory. Same theatre and location as above: 3, 4, 5, 7, 9 September 1908.

333. *The Suburban Groove* by W. F. Casey. Same theatre and location as above: 1, 2, 3 October 1908.

334. *The Piper* by Norreys Connell. Same theatre and location as above: 1, 2, 3 October 1908.

335. *The Clancy Name* by Lennox Robinson. Same theatre and location as above: 8, 9, 10 October 1908.

336. *In the Shadow of the Glen* by John Synge. Same theatre and location as above: 8, 9, 10 October 1908.

337. *Dervorgilla* by Lady Gregory. Same theatre and location as above: 8, 9, 10 October 1908.

338. *The Scheming Lieutenant* by Richard Brinsley Sheridan. Same theatre and location as above: 8, 9, 10 October 1908.

339. *When the Dawn Is Come* by Thomas MacDonagh. The National Theatre Society Ltd., Abbey Theatre, Dublin: 15, 16, 17 October 1908.

340. *The Rogueries of Scapin* by Moliere, translated by Lady Gregory. Same theatre and location as above: 15, 16, 17 October 1908.

341. *The Man Who Missed the Tide* by W. F. Casey. Same theatre and location as above: 22, 23, 24 October 1908.

342. *The Jackdaw* by Lady Gregory. Same theatre and location as above: 22, 23, 24 October 1908.

343. *The Well of Saints* by John Synge. Same theatre and location as above: 29, 30, 31 October 1908.

344. *The Doctor In Spite of Himself* by Moliere, translated by Lady Gregory. Same theatre and location as above: 29, 30, 31 October 1908.

345. *Leaders of the People* by Robert Harding. Ulster Literary Theatre, Exhibition Hall, Belfast: 2, 3, 4, 5, 6, 7 November 1908.

346. *The Drone* by Rutherford Mayne. Same theatre and location as above: 2, 3, 4, 5, 6, 7 November 1908.

347. *The Suburban Groove* by W. F. Casey. The National Theatre Society Ltd., Abbey Theatre, Dublin: 5, 6, 7 November 1908.

348. *The Piper* by Norreys Connell. Same theatre and location as above: 5, 6, 7 November 1908.

349. *Deirdre* by W. B. Yeats. The National Theatre Society Ltd., Abbey Theatre, Dublin: 9, 10, 11 November 1908.

350. *The Rogueries of Scapin* by Moliere, translated by Lady Gregory. Same theatre and location as above: 9, 10, 11 November 1908.

351. *In the Shadow of the Glen* by John Synge. Same theatre and location as above: 14 November 1908.

352. *The Clancy Name* by Lennox Robinson. Same theatre and location as above: 14 November 1908.

353. *The Scheming Lieutenant* by Richard Brinsley Sheridan. Same theatre and location as above: 14 November 1908.

354. *Dervorgilla* by Lady Gregory. Same theatre and location as above: 14 November 1908.

355. *The Pot of Broth* by W. B. Yeats. Same theatre and location as above: 19, 20, 21 November 1908.

356. *The Hour Glass* by W. B. Yeats. Same theatre and location as above: 19, 20, 21 November 1908.

357. *Hyacinth Halvey* by Lady Gregory. Same theatre and location as above: 19, 20, 21 November 1908.

358. *The Rising of the Moon* by Lady Gregory. Same theatre and location as above: 19, 20, 21 November 1908.

359. "Irish play" presented by a Gaelic League Branch, Rotunda Hall, Dublin: 19 November 1908.

360. *The Turn of the Road* by Rutherford Mayne. Cluithcheoiri na hEireann (Theatre of Ireland), Abbey Theatre, Dublin: 23, 24 November 1908.

361. *The Flame on the Hearth* by Seumas O'Kelly. Same theatre and location as above: 23, 24 November 1908.

362. *The Workhouse Ward* by Lady Gregory and Douglas Hyde. The National Theatre Society Ltd., Abbey Theatre, Dublin: 26, 27, 28 November 1908.

363. *The White Cockade* by Lady Gregory. Same theatre and location as above: 26, 27, 28 November 1908.

364. *The Dilettante* by Casimir Dunin Markievicz. The Independent Dramatic Company, Abbey Theatre, Dublin: 3, 4, 5 December 1908.

365. *Home Sweet Home* by Nora Fitzpatrick and Casimir Dunin Markievicz. Same theatre and location as above: 3, 4, 5 December 1908.

366. *The Flame of the Hearth* by Seumas O'Kelly. Cluithcheoiri na hEireann (Theatre of Ireland), Gaiety Theatre, Dublin: early December 1908.

367. *The Turn of the Road* by Rutherford Mayne. Same theatre and location as the above: early December 1908.

368. *Bong Tong Come to Balriddery* by Seumas MacManus. Chapelizod Dramatic Class, location (?) December 1908.

369. *Stella and Vanessa* by Arnold Graves. Irish Theatrical Club, 40 Upper O'Connell Street, Dublin: 10 December 1908.

370. *The Suburban Groove* by W. F. Casey. The National Theatre Society Ltd., Abbey Theatre, Dublin: 26 December 1908.

371. *The Rising of the Moon* by Lady Gregory. Same theatre and location as above: 26 December 1908.

1909

372. *The Gaol Gate* by Lady Gregory. The National Theatre Society Ltd., Abbey Theatre, Dublin: 21, 22, 23, 27, 29, 30 January 1909. The performance on the 23rd was canceled.

373. *The Miser* by Moliere, translated by Lady Gregory. Same theatre and location as above: 21, 22, 23, 27, 29 30 January 1909. The performance on the 23rd was canceled.

374. *The Man Who Missed the Tide* by W. F. Casey. Same theatre and location as above: 4, 5, 6 February 1909.

375. *Kathleen Ni Houlihan* by W. B. Yeats. Same theatre and location as above: 4, 5, 6 February 1909.

376. *Kincora* by Lady Gregory. Same theatre and location as above: 11, 12, 13 February 1909.

377. *The Rising of the Moon* by Lady Gregory. Same theatre and location as above: 11, 12, 13 February 1909.

378. *The Miser* by Moliere, translated by Lady Gregory. Same theatre and location as above: 25, 26, 27 February 1909.

379. *The Gaol Gate* by Lady Gregory. Same theatre and location as above: 25, 26 February 1909.

380. *Kathleen Ni Houlihan* by W. B. Yeats. Same theatre and location as above: 27 February 1909.

381. *A Gallant of Galway* (revised) by James Duncan. Theatre organization (?), for the Dublin Branch of the Women's National Health Association, Abbey Theatre, Dublin: 1 March 1909.

382. *The Suburban Groove* by W. F. Casey. The National Theatre Society Ltd., Abbey Theatre, Dublin: 4, 5, 6 March 1909.

383. *The Pie-dish* by George Fitzmaurice. Same theatre and location as above: 4, 5, 6 March 1909.

384. *Stephen Grey: A Dream and an Incident* by D. L. Kelleher. Same theatre and location as above: 11, 12, 13 March 1909.

385. *The Rogueries of Scapin* by Moliere, translated by Lady Gregory. Same theatre and location as above: 11, 12, 13 March 1909.

386. *An Comhrae* by (?) Colmcille Gaelic League Dramatic Class with actors from the Theatre of Ireland, Rotunda Hall, Dublin: 17 March 1909.

387. *The Man Who Missed the Tide* by W. F. Casey. The National Theatre Society Ltd., Abbey Theater, Dublin: 17, 20 March 1909.

388. *Kathleen Ni Houlihan* by W. B. Yeats. Same theatre and location: 17, 20 March 1909.

389. *The Turn of the Tide* by Rutherford Mayne. Cluithcheoiri na hEireann (Theatre of Ireland), Rotunda Hall, Dublin: 19, 20 March 1909.

390. *The Flame on the Hearth* by Seumas O'Kelly. Same theatre and location as above: 19, 20 March 1909.

391. *The Storm* by Hugh Barden. Metropolitan School of Art Students, Student's Union, Metropolitan School of Art, Dublin: 18 March 1909.

392. *Paid in His Own Coin* by Thomas King Moylan. Same organization and location as above: 18 March 1909.

393. *The Cross Roads* by Lennox Robinson. The National Theatre Society Ltd., Abbey Theatre, Dublin: 25, 26, 27 March and 1, 2, 3 April 1909.

394. *Hyacinth Halvey* by Lady Gregory. Same theatre and location as above: 25, 26, 27 March and 1, 2, 3 April 1909.

395. *Time* by Norreys Connell. Same theatre and location as above: 1, 2, 3 April 1909.

396. *The Suburban Groove* by W. F. Casey. Same theatre and location as above: 12 April 1909.

397. *Kathleen Ni Houlihan* by W. B. Yeats. Same theatre and location as above: 12 April 1909.

398. *The Heather Field* by Edward Martyn. Same theatre and location as above: 15, 16, 17 April 1909.

399. *The Storm* by Hugh Barden. Metropolitan School of Art Students, Abbey Theatre, Dublin: 22, 23, 24 April 1909.

400. *Paid in His Own Coin* by Thomas King Moylan. Same organization and location as above: 22, 23, 24 April 1909.

401. *Kathleen Ni Houlihan* by W. B. Yeats. The National Theatre Society Ltd., Abbey Theatre, Dublin: 29 April 1909.

402. *Hyacinth Halvey* by Lady Gregory. Same theatre and location as above: 29 April 1909.

403. *In the Shadow of the Glen* by John Synge. Same theatre and location as above: 29 April 1909.

404. *The Workhouse Ward* by Lady Gregory and Douglas Hyde. Same theatre and location as above: 29 April 1909.

405. *Kincora* by Lady Gregory. Same theatre and location as above: 29, 30 April 1909.

406. *The Glittering Gate* by Lord Dunsany. Same theatre and location as above: 29, 30 April 1909.

407. *The Shuiler's Child* by Seumas O'Kelly. Cluithcheoiri na hEireann (Theatre of Ireland), Rotunda Hall, Dublin: 29, 30 April and 1 May 1909.

408. *The Gomeril* by Rutherford Mayne. Same theatre and location as above: 29, 30 April and 1 May 1909.

409. *The Cross Roads* by Lennox Robinson. The National Theatre Society Ltd., Abbey Theatre: 6, 7, 8 May 1909.

410. *Time* by Norreys Connell. Same theatre and location as above: 6, 7, 8 May 1909.

411. *The Embers* by Daniel Corkery. The Cork Dramatic Society, Dun Theatre, Queen Street, Cork: 6, 7, May 1909.

412. *The Well of the Saints* by John Synge. The National Theatre Society Ltd., Abbey Theatre, Dublin: 13, 14, 15 May 1909.

413. *An Imaginary Conversation* by Norreys Connell. Same theatre and location as above: 13, 14, 15 May 1909.

414. *In the Shadow of the Glen* by John Synge. Same theatre and location as above: 20, 21, 22 May 1909.

415. *The Glittering Gate* by Lord Dunsany. Same theatre and location as above: 20, 21, 22 May 1909.

416. *Riders to the Sea* by John Synge. Same theatre and location as above: 20, 21, 22 May 1909.

417. *Hyacinth Halvey* by Lady Gregory. Same theatre and location as above: 20, 21, 23 May 1909.

418. *An Imaginary Conversation* by Norreys Connell. Same theatre and location as above: 27, 28, 29 May 1909.

419. *The Playboy of the Western World* by John Synge. Same theatre and location as above: 27, 28, 29 May 1909.

420. Dramatic performance, (play and title are not currently known) by (?). Organization, possibly a Gaelic League Branch (?) for the Feis at New Market, Kilkenny: 29 June 1909.

421. An Irish language play (title is not currently known) by (?). A Gaelic League Branch, Castlebar, County Mayo: 26, 27, 28 July 1909.

422. *Solus na Saoirseactht (The Light Craftsman)* by (?). Same organization and location as above: 26, 27, 28 July 1909.

423. *Deirdre* by Father Kelly (O'Kelly). Ar-Craob Gaelic League Branch and Cluithcheoiri na hEireann (Theatre of Ireland), for the Oireachtas 1909, Rotunda Hall, Dublin: 31 July 1909.

424. *Eithne* an Irish opera, by Robert O'Dwyer and Father Tomas O'Kelly. A Gaelic League Branch (?) for the Oireachtas 1909, Rotunda Hall, Dublin: 2, 3, 5 August 1909.

425. *An Scrabhadoir (The Scratch)* by Tomas O hAodha. "A Specially Selected Company of Native Speakers," possibly a Gaelic League Branch from County Galway, for the Oireachtas 1909, Rotunda Hall, Dublin: 4 August 1909.

426. *The Playboy of the Western World* by John Synge. The National Theatre Society Ltd., Abbey Theatre, Dublin: 24 August 1909.

427. *The Rising of the Moon* by Lady Gregory. Same theatre and location as above: 24 August 1909.

428. *The Shewing up of Blanco Posnet,* by George Bernard Shaw. Same theatre and location as above: 25, 26, 27, 28 August 1909.

This production, and subsequent Dublin Revivals belongs to the Irish Theatre Movement because the National Theatre Society Limited used the play to successfully challenge Dublin Castle, the seat of British rule in Ireland, for the right to perform it after the Lord Chamberlain banned its performance in England.

429. *The Workhouse Ward* by Lady Gregory and Douglas Hyde. Same theatre and location as above: 25, 26, 27, 28 August 1909.

430. *Kathleen Ni Houlihan* by W. B. Yeats. Same theatre and location as above: 25, 26, 27, 28 August 1909.

431. *The Return of Lugh Lamh Fada,* a pageant by Alice Milligan. National Council, County Dublin: 25, 26 August 1909.

432. *The White Feather* by R. J. Ray (R. G. Brophy). The National Theatre Society Ltd., Abbey Theatre, Dublin: 16, 17, 18 September 1909.

433. *Spreading the News* by Lady Gregory. Same theatre and location as above: 16, 17, 18 September 1909.

434. *The Man Who Missed the Tide* by W. F. Casey. Same theatre and location as above: 23, 24, 25 September 1909.

435. *The Piper* by Norreys Connell. Same theatre and location as above: 23, 24, 25 September 1909.

436. *The Shewing Up of Blanco Posnet* by George Bernard Shaw. Same theatre and location as above: 30 September and 1, 2 October 1909.

437. *The Clancy Name* by Lennox Robinson. Same theatre and location as above: 30 September and 1, 2 October 1909.

438. *The Workhouse Ward* by Lady Gregory and Douglas Hyde. Same theatre and location as above: 30 September and 1, 2 October 1909.

439. *The Cross Roads* by Lennox Robinson. Same theatre and location as above: 7, 8, 9 October 1909.

440. *The Rising of the Moon* by Lady Gregory. Same theatre and location as above: 7, 8, 9 October 1909.

441. *The Challenge* by Winifred M. Letts. Same theatre and location as above: 14, 15, 16 October 1909.

442. *The Suburban Groove* by W. F. Casey. Same theatre and location as above: 14, 15, 16 October 1909.

443. *Spreading the News* by Lady Gregory. Same theatre and location as above: 21 October 1909.

444. *Riders to the Sea* by John Synge. Same theatre and location as above: 21, 22, 23 October 1909.

445. *The Workhouse Ward* by Lady Gregory and Douglas Hyde. Same theatre and location as above: 21, 22, 23 October 1909.

446. *The Miser* by Moliere, translated by Lady Gregory. Same theatre and location as above: 21, 22, 23 October 1909.

447. *The Shewing Up of Blanco Posnet* by George Bernard Shaw. Same theatre and location as above: 28, 29, 30 October 1909.

448. *The Jackdaw* by Lady Gregory. Same theatre and location as above: 28, 29 30 October 1909.

449. *The Glittering Gate* by Lord Dunsany. Same theatre and location as above: 29, 30 October 1909.

450. *Irish Tableaux Vivants.* Inghinidhe na hEireann Dramatic Classes, Rotunda Hall, Dublin: 1 November 1909.

451. *The Pot of Broth* by W. B. Yeats. The National Theatre Society Ltd., Abbey Theatre, Dublin: 4, 5, 6 November 1909.

452. *The Hour Glass* by W. B. Yeats. Same theatre and location as above: 4, 5, 6 November 1909.

453. *The Building Fund* by William Boyle. Same theatre and location as above: 4, 5, 6 November 1909.

454. *The Image* by Lady Gregory. Same theatre and location as above: 11, 12, 13 November 1909.

455. *The Rising of the Moon* by Lady Gregory. Same theatre and location as above: 11, 12, 13 November 1909.

456. *The Shuiler's Child* by Seumas O'Kelly. Cluithcheoiri na hEireann (Theatre of Ireland), Rotunda Hall, Dublin: 11, 13 November 1909.

457. *The Matchmakers* by Seumas O'Kelly. Same theatre and location as above: 11, 13 November 1909.

458. *Deirdre* by Father Kelly. Same theatre and location as above: 11, 13 November 1909.

459. *Kathleen Ni Houlihan* by W. B. Yeats. The National Theatre Society Ltd., Abbey Theatre, Dublin: 18, 19, 20 November 1909.

460. *The Shewing Up of Blanco Posnet* by George Bernard Shaw. Same theatre and location as above: 18, 19, 20 November 1909.

461. *The Workhouse Ward* by Lady Gregory and Douglas Hyde. Same theatre and location as above: 18, 19, 20 November 1909.

462. The *Drone* by Rutherford Mayne. The Ulster Literary Theatre, Abbey Theatre, Dublin: 26, 27 November 1909.

463. *The Mist That Does Be on the Bog* by Gerald MacNamara. Same theatre and location as above: 26, 27 November 1909.

464. *The Wheel O'Fortune* by T. C. Murray. The Cork Dramatic Society, Dun Theatre, Queen Street, Cork: 2, 3 (maybe 4) December 1909.

465. *The Hermit and the King* by Daniel Corkery. Same theatre and location as above: 2, 3 (maybe 4) December 1909.

466. *The Lesson of His Life* by Lennox Robinson. Same theatre and location as above: 2, 3 (maybe 4) December 1909.

467. *The Eloquent Dempsey* by William Boyle. The Pioneer Dramatic Society, St. Francis Xaviers Hall, Dublin: 14, 15 December 1909.

1910

468. *The Pot of Broth* by W. B. Yeats. The National Theatre Society Ltd., Abbey Theatre, Dublin: 6, 7, 8 January 1910.

469. *The Gaol Gate* by Lady Gregory. Same theatre and location as above: 6, 7, 8 January 1910.

470. *The Building Fund* by William Boyle. Same theatre and location as above: 6, 7, 8 January 1910.

471. *Deirdre of the Sorrows* by John Synge. Same theatre and location as above: 13, 14, 15 January 1910.

    This play, unfinished when Synge died, was first billed as *The Sorrows of Deirdre*.

472. *The Rising Moon* by Lady Gregory. Same theatre and location as above: 13, 14, 15 January 1910.

473. *Interior* by Maurice Maeterlinck. Same theatre and location as above: 20, 21, 22 January 1910.

474. *The Canavans* by Lady Gregory. Same theatre and location as above: 20, 21, 22, January 1910.

475. *The Cross Roads* by Lennox Robinson. Same theatre and location as above: 3, 4, 5 February 1910.

476. *The Doctor In Spite of Himself* by Moliere, translated by Lady Gregory. Same theatre and location as above: 3, 4, 5 February 1910.

477. *Destruction of Da Derga's Hostel* by Padraic Colum St. Enda's School Theatre, St. Enda's School County Dublin: 5, 6, February 1910.

    St. Enda's was Padraic Pearse's school. Its theatrical productions were staged by Pearse, his brother William, Thomas MacDonagh, or by a collaboration of the above. While the actors were mostly students, some adults regularly appeared in their plays.

478. *Iosagan* by Padraic Pearse. Same theatre and location as above: 5, 6, February 1910. (Iosagan is the Gaelicization of Jesus.)

479. *The Green Helmet* by W. B. Yeats. The National Theatre Society Ltd., Abbey Theatre, Dublin: 10, 11, 12 February 1910.

480. *The Playboy of the Western World* by John Synge. Same theatre and location as above: 10, 11, 12 February 1910.

481. *Deirdre* by W. B. Yeats. Same theatre and location as above: 17, 18, 19 February 1910.

482. *The Workhouse Ward* by Lady Gregory and Douglas Hyde. Same theatre and location as above: 17, 18, 19 February 1910.

483. *The Shewing Up of Blanco Posnet* by George Bernard Shaw. Same theatre and location as above: 17, 18, 19 February 1910.

484. *The True Born Irishman* by Charles Macklin. Cluithcheoiri na hEireann (Theatre of Ireland), Molesworth Hall Dublin: 18, 19 February 1910.

    Macklin's script was adapted for this production, however, the adapter is not known.

485. *Expiation* by Kathleen Fitzpatrick. Same theatre and location as above: 18, 19 February 1910.

486. *Mirandolina* by Carlo Goldini translated by Lady Gregory. The National Theatre Society Ltd., Abbey Theatre, Dublin: 24, 25, 26 February 1910.

487. *The Traveling Man* by Lady Gregory. Same theatre and location as above: 3, 4, 5 March 1910.

488. *The Image* by Lady Gregory. Same theatre and location as above: 3, 4, 5 March 1910.

489. *The Flame on the Earth* by (?). Cluithcheoiri na hEireann (Theatre of Ireland), Banba Hall 5 March 1910.

490. *The Mist That Does Be On the Bog* by Gerald MacNamara. The Ulster Literary Theatre, Grand Opera House, Belfast: 7 March 1910.

491. *The Drone* by Rutherford Mayne. Same theatre and location as above: 7, 9 March 1910.

492. *Captain of the Hosts* by Rutherford Mayne. Same theatre and location as above: 8 March 1910.

493. *The Naming of Cuchullain* by Sir Samuel Ferguson. Same theatre and location as above: 9 March 1910.

494. *The Man Who Missed the Tide* by W. F. Casey. The National Theatre Society Ltd., Abbey Theatre, Dublin: 10, 11, 12 March 1910.

495. *The Jackdaw* by Lady Gregory. Same theatre and location as above: 10, 11, 12 March 1910.

496. *Hyacinth Halvey* by Lady Gregory. Same theatre and location as above: 17, 18, 19 March 1910.

497. *In the Shadow of the Glen* by John Synge. Same theatre and location as above: 17, 18, 19 March 1910.

498. *The Building Fund* by William Boyle. Same theatre and location as above: 17, 18, 19 March 1910.

499. *Deirdre* by W. B. Yeats. Same theatre and location as above: 28, 29, 30, 31 March 1910.

500. *The Workhouse Ward* by Lady Gregory and Douglas Hyde. Same theatre and location as above: 28, 29, 30, 31 March 1910.

501. *The Shewing Up of Blanco Posnet* by George Bernard Shaw. Same theatre and location as above: 28, 29, 30, 31 March 1910.

502. *The Spurious Queen* by J. O'E. Cluithcheoiri na hEireann (Theatre of Ireland), Molesworth Hall, Dublin: 28, 30, 31 March and 2 April 1910.

503. *The Home Coming* by Seumas O'Kelly. Same theatre and location as above: 28, 30, 31 March and 2 April 1910.

504. *The Tinker and the Fairy* an operetta with lyrics by Douglas Hyde. The Dublin Amateur Operatic Society, Dublin: 27 March 1910.

505. *The Glittering Gate* by Lord Dunsany. The National Theatre Society Ltd., Abbey Theatre, Dublin: 1, 2 April 1910.

506. *The Eloquent Dempsey* by William Boyle. Same theatre and location as above: 1, 2 April 1910.

507. *An Naomh ar Iarraid (The Lost Saint)* by Douglas Hyde. St. Enda's School Theatre, Abbey Theatre, Dublin: 9 April 1910.

508. *The Destruction of da Derga's Hostel* by Padraic Colum Same theatre and location as above: 9 April 1910.

509. *Iosagan* by Padraic Pearse. Same theatre and location as above: 9 April 1910.

510. *The Coming of Fionn* by Standish O'Grady. Same theatre and location as above: 9 April 1910.

511. *The Memory of the Dead* by Casimir Dunin Markievicz. The Independent Dramatic Company, Abbey Theatre, Dublin: 14, 16 April 1910.

512. *Mary* by Casimir Dunin Markievicz. Same theatre and location as above: 14, 16 April 1910.

513. *Deirdre of the Sorrows* by John Synge. The National Theatre Society, Abbey Theatre, Dublin: 28, 29, 30 April 1910.

514. *The Jackdaw* by Lady Gregory. Same theatre and location as above: 28, 29, 30 April 1910.

515. *Thomas Muskerry* by Padraic Colum. Same theatre and location as above: 5, 6, 7 May 1910.

516. *A Pot of Broth* by W. B. Yeats. Same theatre and location as above: 5, 6, 7 May 1910.

517. *Struck* by Con O'Leary. The Cork Dramatic Society, Dun Theatre, Cork: 11, 12, 13 May 1910.

518. *The Burden* by E. K Worthington. Same theatre and location as above: 11, 12, 13 May 1910.

519. *The Eloquent Dempsey* by William Boyle. The National Theatre Society Ltd., Abbey Theatre, Dublin: 12, 13, 14 May 1910.

520. *The Glittering Gate* by Lord Dunsany. Same theatre and location as above: 12, 13, 14 May 1910.

521. *Eithne* an Irish opera by Robert O'Dwyer and Father Tomas O'Kelly. The Dublin Amateur Opera Society (?) Gaiety Theater, Dublin: 16 May 1910.

522. *The Coming of Aideen* by Mary Costello. The Irish Theatrical Club, 40 Upper O'Connell Street, Dublin: 18 May 1910.

523. *The Gods at Play* by Mary Costello. Same theatre and location as above: 18 May 1910.

524. *Harvest* by Lennox Robinson. The National Theatre Society Ltd., Abbey Theatre, Dublin: 19, 20, 21 May 1910.

525. *The Green Helmet* by W. B. Yeats. Same theatre and location as above: 19, 20, 21 May 1910.

526. *The Memory of the Dead* by Casimir Dunin Markievicz. The Independent Dramatic Company, Gaiety Theatre, Dublin: 23 May 1910.

527. *Home Sweet Home* by Nora Fitzpatrick and Casimir Dunin Markievicz. Same theatre and location as above: 23 May 1910.

528. *The Message* by M. B. Pearse. The Leinster Stage Society Theatre, Dublin: 28 May 1910.

M. B. Pearse was Margaret Pearse, a sister of Padraic and William Pearse. She and William formed the Leinster Stage Society.

529.   *The Naboclish* by Thomas King Moylan. Metropolitan School of Art Students, Abbey Theatre, Dublin: 31 May 1910.

530.   *Cuaird na Bainroghna (The Queen's Visit)* by W. P. Ryan. The Keating Branch of the Gaelic League, for the Oireachtas 1910, Rotunda Hall, Dublin: 4 August 1910.

531.   *Aine agus Caoimhin (Annie and Kevin)* by Tomas Mac Domhnaill. Cluithcheoiri na hEireann (Theatre of Ireland), for the Oireachtas 1910, Rotunda Hall, Dublin: 4 August 1910.

532.   *An tOide as Tir na nOg (The Teacher from Tir na nOg)* by W. P. Ryan. The Keating Branch of the Gaelic League, for the Oireachtas 1910, Rotunda Hall, Dublin: 4 August 1910.

533.   *Oighreacht Roisin (The Inheritance of Roisin)* by Padraic O Seaghda. Same organization and location as above: 5 August 1910.

534.   *An tSnaihm (The Knot)* by Alponr O Ladpraid. Same organization and location as above: 5 August 1910.

535.   *Hyacinth Halvey* by Lady Gregory. The National Theatre Society Ltd., Abbey Theatre, Dublin: 22, 23, 24, 25, 26, 27 August 1910.

536.   *The Cross Roads* by Lennox Robinson. Same theatre and location as above: 22, 23, 24, 25, 26, 27 August 1910.

537.   *The Rising of the Moon* by Lady Gregory. Same theatre and location as above: 22, 23, 24, 25, 26, 27 August 1910.

538.   *The Playboy of the Western World* by John Synge. Same theatre and location as above: 24, 25 August 1910.

539.   *Kathleen Ni Houlihan* by W. B. Yeats. Same theatre and location as above: 24, 25 August 1910.

540.   *The Shewing Up of Blanco Posnet* by George Bernard Shaw. Same theatre and location as above: 25, 26, 27 August 1910.

541.   *The Building Fund* by William Boyle. Same theatre and location as above: 25, 26, 27 August 1910.

542. *Riders to the Sea* by John Synge. Same theatre and location as above: 8, 9, 10 September 1910.

543. *The Mineral Workers* by William Boyle. Same theatre and location as above: 8, 9, 10 September 1910.

544. *The Gaol Gate* by Lady Gregory. Same theatre and location as above: 15, 16, 17 September 1910.

545. *The Suburban Groove* by W. F. Casey. Same theatre and location as above: 15, 16, 17 September 1910.

546–554. Nine Gaelic language plays were performed in Dublin (probably by a Gaelic League Branch theatre), mid-September 1910. Specific titles, authors, organization, location, and dates are currently unknown.

555. *The Well of Saints* by John Synge. Same theatre and location as above: 22, 23, 24 September 1910.

556. *The Piper* by Norreys Connell. Same theatre and location as above: 22, 23, 24 September 1910.

557. *The Casting Out of Martin Whelan* by R. J. Ray. Same theatre and location as above: 29, 30 September and 1 October 1910.

558. *The Workhouse Ward* by Lady Gregory and Douglas Hyde. Same theatre and location as above: 29, 30 September and 1 October 1910.

559. *The Man Who Missed the Tide* by W. F. Casey. Same theatre and location as above: 29, 30 September and 1 October 1910.

560. *The Bailiff of Kilmore* by Joseph Ford. The New Ireland Dramatic Society, Molseworth Hall: 10, 11 October 1910.

561. *The Call to Arms* by Peter Kearney. Same theatre and location as above: 10, 11 October 1910.

562. *Teig Corcoran's Courtship* by James Cregan. Same theatre and location as above: 10, 11 October 1910.

563. *Thomas Muskerry* by Padraic Colum. The National Theatre Society Ltd., Abbey Theatre, Dublin: 13, 14, 15 October 1910.

564. *The Rising of the Moon* by Lady Gregory. Same theatre and location as above: 13, 14, 15 October 1910.

565. *The Glittering Gate* by Lord Dunsany. Same theatre and location as above: 20, 21, 22 October 1910.

566. *The Miser* by Moliere, translated by Lady Gregory. Same theatre and location as above: 20, 21, 22 October 1910.

567. *Spreading the News* by Lady Gregory. Same theatre and location as above: 27, 28, 29 October 1910.

568. *Birthright* by T. C. Murray. Same theatre and location as above: 27, 28, 29 October 1910.

569. *The Rising of the Moon* by Lady Gregory. Same theatre and location as above: 27, 28, 29 October 1910.

570. *The Embers* by Daniel Corkery. Cork Dramatic Society, Dun Theatre, Cork: 2, 3, 4 November 1910.

571. *The Last Warriors* by Terence MacSwiney. Same theatre and location as above: 2, 3, 4 November 1910.

572. *Interior* by Maurice Maeterlinck. The National Theatre Society Ltd., Abbey Theatre, Dublin: 3, 4, 5 November 1910.

573. *The Mineral Workers* by William Boyle. Same theatre and location as above: 3, 4, 5 November 1910.

574. *An tOide as Tir na nOg (The Teacher from Tir na nOg)* by W. P. Ryan. The Keating Branch of the Gaelic League, Abbey Theatre, Dublin: 7 November 1910.

575. *The Cross Roads* by Lennox Robinson. The National Theatre Society Ltd., Abbey Theatre, Dublin: 10, 11, 12 November 1910.

576. *Full Moon* by Lady Gregory. Same theatre and location as above: 10, 11, 12 November 1910.

577. *Riders to the Sea* by John Synge. Same theatre and location as above: 17, 18, 19 November 1910.

578. *Mirandolina* by Carlo Goldini, translated by Lady Gregory. Same theatre and location as above: 17, 18, 19 November 1910.

579. *The Pie-dish* by George Fitzmaurice. Same theatre and location as above: 24, 25, 26 November 1910.

580. *The Shuiler's Child* by Seumas O'Kelly. Same theatre and location as above: 24, 25, 26 November 1910.

581. *Hyacinth Halvey* by Lady Gregory. Same theatre and location as above: 24, 25, 26 November 1910.

582. *The Shewing Up of Blanco Posnet* by George Bernard Shaw. Same theatre and location as above: 1, 2, 3 December 1910.

583. *Coats* by Lady Gregory. Same theatre and location as above: 1, 2, 3 December 1910.

584. *The Building Fund* by William Boyle. Same theatre and location as above: 1, 2, 3 December 1910.

585. *The Clancy Name* by Lennox Robinson. Same theatre and location as above: 8, 9, 10 December 1910.

586. *The Eloquent Dempsey* by William Boyle. Same theatre and location as above: 8, 9, 10 December 1910.

587. *The Mineral Workers* by William Boyle. Same theatre and location as above: 26, 28, 30 December 1910.

588. *The Rising of the Moon* by Lady Gregory. Same theatre and location as above: 26, 28, 30 December 1910.

589. *In the Shadow of the Glen* by John Synge. Same theatre and location as above: 27, 29, 31 December 1910.

590. *The Suburban Groove* by W. F. Casey. Same theatre and location as above: 27, 29, 31 December 1910.

591. *A Daughter of Ireland* by George J. Hurson. The Pioneer Dramatic Society, St, Francis Xavier's Hall, Dublin: 26 (and possibly more dates) December 1910.

592. *The Hermit and the King* by Daniel Corkery. The Cork Dramatic Society, Dun Theatre, Cork: 27, 28, 29 December 1910.

593. *The Lesson of His Life* by Lennox Robinson. Same theatre and location as above: 27, 28, 29 December 1910.

594. *The Holocaust* by Terence MacSwiney. Same theatre and location as above: 27, 28, 29 December 1910.

1911

595. *A Nativity Play* by Douglas Hyde, translated by Lady Gregory. The National Theatre Society Ltd., Abbey Theatre, Dublin: 5, 6, 7 January 1911.

596. *The Rogueries of Scapin* by Moliere, translated by Lady Gregory. Same theatre and location as above: 5, 6, 7 January 1911.

597. *Kathleen Ni Houlihan* by W. B. Yeats. Same theatre and location as above: 5, 6, 7 January 1911.

598. *The Hour Glass* by W. B. Yeats. Same theatre and location as above: 13, 14, 15 January 1911.

599. *The Deliverer* by Lady Gregory. Same theatre and location as above: 13, 14, 15 January 1911.

600. *The Full Moon* by Lady Gregory. Same theatre and location as above: 13, 14, 15 January 1911.

601. *Harvest* by Lennox Robinson. Same theatre and location as above: 19, 20, 21 January 1911.

602. *The Jackdaw* by Lady Gregory. Same theatre and location as above: 19, 20, 21 January 1911.

603. *King Argimenes and the Unknown Warrior* by Lord Dunsany. Same theatre and location as above: 26, 27, 28 January 1911.

604. *The Man Who Missed the Tide* by W. F. Casey. Same theatre and location as above: 26, 27, 28 January 1911.

605. *Deirdre* by W. B. Yeats. Same theatre and location as above: 2, 3, 4 February 1911.

606. *The Cross Roads* by Lennox Robinson. Same theatre and location as above: 2, 3, 4 February 1911.

607. *Coats* by Lady Gregory. Same theatre and location as above: 2, 3, 4 February 1911.

608. *The Image* by Lady Gregory. Same theatre and location as above: 9, 10, 11, February 1911.

609. *The Piper* by Norreys Connell. Same theatre and location as above: 9, 10, 11 February 1911.

610. *The Storm* by Ostrovosky. Cluithcheoiri na hEireann (Theatre of Ireland), Molesworth Hall, Dublin: 20, 21 February 1911.

611. *The Land of Heart's Desire* by W. B. Yeats. The National Theatre Society Ltd., Abbey Theatre, Dublin: 16, 17, 18 February 1911.

612. *Birthright* by T. C. Murray. Same theatre and location as above: 16, 17, 18 February 1911.

613. *A Pot of Broth* by W. B. Yeats. Same theatre and location as above: 16, 17, 18 February 1911.

614. *The Cricket on the Hearth* by M. B. Pearse. The Leinster Stage Society, Abbey Theatre, Dublin: 23, 24, 25 February 1911.

615. *The Skull* by Morgan O'Friel. Same theatre and location as above: 23, 24, 25 February 1911.

616. *The Racing Lug* by James Cousins. Same theatre and location as above: 23, 24, 25 February 1911.

617. *Deirdre* by AE. Same theatre and location as above: 23, 24, 25 February 1911.

618. *Down in Kerry* by Brian MacCarthy. Ui Breasail Amateur Dramatic Society, Abbey Theatre: 28 February 1911.

619. *The Pie-dish* by George Fitzmaurice. The National Theatre Society Ltd., Abbey Theatre, Dublin: 2, 3, 4 March 1911.

620. *The Eloquent Dempsey* by William Boyle. Same theatre and location as above: 2, 3, 4 March 1911.

621. *Thomas Muskerry* by Padraic Colum. Same theatre and location as above: 9, 10, 11 March 1911.

622. *The Workhouse Ward* by Lady Gregory and Douglas Hyde. Same theatre and location as above: 9, 10, 11 March 1911.

623. *The True Born Irishman* by Charles Macklin. Cluithcheoiri na hEireann (Theatre of Ireland), Molesworth Hall, Dublin: 17 March 1911.

624. *In the Shadow of the Glen* by John Synge. The National Theatre Society Ltd., Abbey Theatre, Dublin: 16, 17, 18 March 1911.

625. *The Mineral Workers* by William Boyle. Same theatre and location as above: 16, 17, 18 March 1911.

626. *The Rising of the Moon* by Lady Gregory. Same theatre and location as above: 23, 24, 25 March 1911.

627. *The Building Fund* by William Boyle. Same theatre and location as above: 23, 24, 25 March 1911.

628. *The Glittering Gate* by Lord Dunsany. Same theatre and location as above: 23, 24, 25 March 1911.

629. *Mixed Marriage* by St. John Ervine. Same theatre and location as above: 30 March and 1 April 1911.

630. *A Passion Play* by Padraic Pearse. St. Enda's School and St. Ita's School Theatre, Abbey Theatre, Dublin: 7, 8 April 1911.

631. *The Memory of the Dead* by Casimir Dunin Markievicz. The Independent Dramatic Company, Queen's Theatre, Dublin: 15 April 1911.

632. *Kathleen Ni Houlihan* by W. B. Yeats. The National Theatre Society Ltd., Abbey Theatre, Dublin: 17, 18, 21, 22 April 1911.

633. *Mixed Marriage* by St. John Ervine. Same theatre and location as above: 17, 18, 21, 22 April 1911.

634. *The Man Who Missed the Tide* by W. F. Casey. Same theatre and location as above: 19, 20, 22 April 1911.

635. *Deirdre* by W. B. Yeats. Same theatre and location as above: 19, 20, 22 April 1911.

636. *The Onus of Ownership* by Daniel Corkery. The Cork Dramatic Society, Dun Theatre, Cork: 19, 20, 21 April 1911.

637. *Manners Maketh Man* by Terence MacSwiney. Same theatre and location as above: 19 20, 21 April 1911.

638. *The Last Warriors of Coole* by Terence MacSwiney. Same theatre and location as above: 19, 20, 21 April 1911.

639. Possibly five additional plays were presented by the Cork Dramatic Society at this time, but their specific titles are not presently known.

640. *A Daughter of Ireland* by George Hurson. The Pioneer Dramatic Society, St. Francis Xavier Hall, Dublin: 17, 19, 21 April 1911.

641. *The West's Awake* by Joseph M. (J. Malachi Muldoon). Same theatre and location as above: 17, 19, 21 April 1911.

642. *Riders to the Sea* by John Synge. The National Theatre Society Ltd., Abbey Theatre, Dublin: 29 April 1911.

643. *The Playboy of the Western World* by John Synge. Same theatre and location as above: 29 April 1911.

644. *The Glittering Gate* by Lord Dunsany. Same theatre and location as above: 25, 29 April 1911.

645. *The Eloquent Dempsey* by William Boyle. Same theatre and location as above: 25, 29 April 1911.

646. *The Shewing Up of Blanco Posnet* by George Bernard Shaw. Same theatre and location as above: 28, 29 April 1911.

647. *The Cross Roads* by Lennox Robinson. Same theatre and location as above: 28, 29 April 1911.

648. *The Rising of the Moon* by Lady Gregory. Same theatre and location as above: 28, 29 April 1911.

649. *The Holocaust* by Terence MacSwiney. The Cork Dramatic Society, Dun Theatre, Cork: 18, 19 May 1911.

650. *The Lesson of His Life* by Lennox Robinson. Same theatre and location as above: 18, 19 May 1911.

651. *The Epilogue* by Daniel Corkery. Same theatre and location as above: 18, 19 May 1911.

652. *Honor's Choice* by Johanna Redmond. The Irish Theatre and National Stage Society, Dublin: 26 July 1911.

653. An Irish language play (title is not currently known) by Maire Ni Chinneide. A Gaelic League Branch, for the Oireachtas 1911, Rotunda Hall, Dublin: 31 July 1911.

654. *Seaghan na Scuab (The Tale of the Broom)* by T. O hAodha. Same organization and location as above: 4 August 1911.

655. *An Tincear agus an tSidheog (The Tinker and the Sheeog) by* Douglas Hyde. Same organization and location as above: 5 August 1911.

656. *A Feis at Ancient Tara* a pageant by (?). Same organization and location as above: 5 August 1911.

657. *Kathleen Ni Houlihan* by W. B. Yeats. The National Theatre Society Ltd., Abbey Theatre, Dublin: 21, 26 August 1911.

658. *The Eloquent Dempsey* by William Boyle. Same theatre and location as above: 21, 26 August 1911.

659. *In the Shadow of the Glen* by John Synge. Same theatre and location as above: 22, 24 August 1911.

660. *Birthright* by T. C. Murray. Same theatre and location as above: 22, 24, 31 August 1911.

661. *The Jackdaw* by Lady Gregory. Same theatre and location as above: 22, 23, 24, 25 August 1911.

662. *The Cross Roads* by Lennox Robinson. Same theatre and location as above: 23, 25 August 1911.

663. *The Piper* by Norreys Connell. Same theatre and location as above: 23, 25 August 1911.

664. *The Workhouse Ward* by Lady Gregory and Douglas Hyde. Same theatre and location as above: 23, 25 August 1911.

665. *Harvest* by Lennox Robinson. Same theatre and location as above: 28, 29, 30 August and 1, 2 September 1911.

666. *Hyacinth Halvey* by Lady Gregory. Same theatre and location as above: 31 August 1911.

667. *The Rising of the Moon* by Lady Gregory. Same theatre and location as above: 31 August and 1, 2 September 1911.

668. *The Love Charm* by William Boyle. Same theatre and location as above: 4 September 1911.

669. *Pro Patria* by Johanna Redmond. The Irish Theatre and National Stage Society, Queen's Theatre, Dublin: 4, 5, 6, 7, 8, 9 September 1911.

670. *The Coming of Ardeen* by Mary Costello. Same theatre and location as above: 4, 5, 6, 7, 8, 9 September 1911.

671. *The Hospital Ward* by J. Malachi Muldoon. Same theatre and location as above: 4, 5, 6, 7, 8, 9, September 1911.

672. *The Pie-dish* by George Fitzmaurice. The National Theatre Society Ltd., Abbey Theatre, Dublin: 5, 9 September 1911.

673. *The Well of Saints* by John Synge. The same theatre and location as above: 5, 9 September 1911.

674. *Deirdre* by W. B. Yeats. Same theatre and location as above: 8 September 1911.

675. *The Shewing Up of Blanco Posnet* by George Bernard Shaw. Same theatre and location as above: 8 September 1911.

676. *The Clancy Name* by Lennox Robinson. Same theatre and location as above: 9 September 1911.

677. *The Mineral Workers* by William Boyle. Same theatre and location as above: 9 September 1911.

678. *The Interlude of Youth* by Anon. The Abbey School of Acting, the National Theatre Society Ltd., Abbey Theatre, Dublin: 16 November 1911.

679. *The Marriage* by Douglas Hyde, translated by Lady Gregory. Same theatre and location as above: 16 November 1911.

680. *The Turn of the Road* by Rutherford Mayne. Cluithcheoiri na hEireann (Theatre of Ireland), Hardwicke Street Hall, Dublin: 16, 17, 18 November 1911.

681. *The Marriage of Julia Elizabeth* by James Stephens. Same theatre and location as above: 16, 17, 18 November 1911.

682. *The Second Shepard's Play* by Anon. The Abbey School of Acting, the National Theatre Society Ltd., Abbey Theatre, Dublin: 23 November 1911.

683. *Charity* by Molly F. Scott. The Ulster Literary Theatre, Grand Opera House, Belfast: 4 (and possibly more dates) December 1911.

684. *The Drone* by Rutherford Mayne. Same theatre and location as above: 4 (and possibly more dates) December 1911.

685. *The Enthusiast* by Lewis Purcell. Same theatre and location as above: 4 (and possibly more dates) December 1911.

686. *Red Turf* by Rutherford Mayne. Same theatre and location as above: 5 (and possibly more dates) December 1911.

687. *The Jerrybuilder's* by William Paul. Same theatre and location as above: 5 (and possibly more dates) December 1911.

688. *The Onus of Ownership* by Daniel Corkery. The Cork Dramatic Society, Dun Theatre, Cork: 6, 7, 8 December 1911.

689. *The Wooing of Emer* by Terence MacSwiney. Same theatre and location as above: 6, 7, 8 December 1911.

690. *The Countess Cathleen* by W. B. Yeats. The Abbey School of Acting, the National Theatre Society Ltd., Abbey Theatre, Dublin: 14, 15, 16 December 1911.

691. *The Second Shepard's Play* by Anon. The Same theatre and location as above: 14, 15, 16 December 1911.

692. *Eleanor's Enterprise* by George A. Birmingham. The Independent Theatre Company (formerly the Independent Dramatic Company), Gaiety Theatre, Dublin: 12, 14, 16 December 1911.

693. *Rival Stars* by Casimir Dunin Markievicz. Same theatre and location as above: 11, 13, 15, 16 December 1911.

694. *A Bunch of Lavenda* by James Barlow. Cluithcheoiri na hEireann (Theatre of Ireland), Hardwick Street Hall, Dublin: 18, 19 December 1911.

695. *The Widow Dempsey's Funeral* by Watty Cox. Same theatre and location as above: 18, 19 December 1911.

696. *The Racing Lug* by James Cousins. The Leinster Stage Society, Abbey Theatre, Dublin: 26 December 1911.

697. *The Skull* by Morgan O'Friel. Same theatre and location as above: 26 December 1911.

698. *The Good People* by M. B. Pearse. Same theatre and location as above: 26 December 1911.

699. *For a Lady's Sake* by Seumas O'Heran. Same theatre and location as above: 26 December 1911.

1912

700. *The Annunciation* by Anon. The Abbey School of Acting, the National Theatre Society Ltd., Abbey Theatre, Dublin: 4 January 1912.

701. *The Flight into Egypt* by Anon. Same theatre and location as above: 4 January 1912.

702. *MacDaragh's Wife* (later re-titled *McDonogh's Wife*) by Lady Gregory. Same theatre and location as above: 11 January 1912.

703. *The Workhouse Ward* by Lady Gregory and Douglas Hyde. Same theatre and location as above: 11 January 1912.

704. *Red Turf* by Rutherford Mayne. Same theatre and location as above: 11 January 1912.

705. *The Building Fund* by William Boyle. Same theatre and location as above: 18 January 1912.

706. *Dervorgilla* by Lady Gregory. Same theatre and location as above: 18 January 1912.

707. *The Rising of the Moon* by Lady Gregory. Same theatre and location as above: 18 January 1912.

708. *Grangecolman* by Edward Martyn. The Independent Theatre Company, Abbey Theatre, Dublin: 25, 26, 27 January 1912.

709. *Unseen Kings (The Enchantment of Cuchullain)* by Eva Gore-Booth. Same theatre and location as above: 25, 26, 27 January 1912.

710. *Leap Year* by Johanna Redmond. The Aughrim National School, (?): 4 February 1912.

711. *Spreading the News* by Lady Gregory. Abbey School of Acting, the National Theatre Society Ltd., Abbey Theatre, Dublin: 8 February 1912.

712. *An Tincear agus an tSidheog (The Tinker and the Sheeog)* by Douglas Hyde. Same theatre and location as above: 8 February 1912.

713. *The Canavans* by Lady Gregory. Same theatre and location as above: 8 February 1912.

714. *Dubhairt se Dabhairt se* (Irish translation of *Spreading the News*) by Lady Gregory, translated by An Seabhac. The Clapham School, Clapham Reform Club, Clapham: 17 February 1912.

715. *The Memory of the Dead* by Casimir Dunin Markievicz. The Independent Theatre Company, Cork Opera House, Cork: 19 (and possibly 20) February 1912.

716. *The Dangerous Age* by Nora Fitzpatrick. Same theatre and location as above: 19 (and possibly 20) February 1912.

717. *The Land of Heart's Desire* by W. B. Yeats. Abbey School of Acting, the National Theatre Society Ltd., Abbey Theatre, Dublin: 22, 23, 24 February 1912.

718. *The Rising of the Moon* by Lady Gregory. Same theatre and location as above: 22, 23, 24 February 1912.

719. *Caitlin Ni hCallahain* (Irish translation of *Kathleen Ni Houlihan*) by W. B. Yeats, translated by Father Kelly. Gaelic League Branch of the Five Provinces, Dublin: 24 February 1912.

720. An Irish language play (title is not currently known) by (?) Same organization as above: 24 February 1912.

721. *The World and the Chylde* by Anon. The Abbey School of Acting, the National Theatre Society Ltd., Abbey Theatre, Dublin: 29 February 1912.

722. *In the Shadow of the Glen* by John Synge. The National Theatre Society Ltd., Abbey Theatre, Dublin: 14, 15, 16 March 1912.

723. *Birthright* by T. C. Murray. Same theatre and location as above: 14, 15, 16 March 1912.

724. *The Workhouse Ward* by Lady Gregory and Douglas Hyde. Same theatre and location as above: 14, 15, 16 February 1912.

725. *O'Donnell's Cross* by L. MacManus. The Pioneer Dramatic Club, St. Francis Xavier Hall, Dublin: 18 March 1912.

726. *Leap Year* by Johanna Redmond. Same theatre and location as above: 18 March 1912.

727. *A Pot of Broth* by W. B. Yeats. The National Theatre Society Ltd., Second Company, Abbey Theatre, Dublin: 19 March 1912.

728. *The Mineral Workers* by William Boyle. Same theatre and location as above: 19 March 1912.

729. *Family Failing* by William Boyle. Same theatre and location as above: 28, 29, 30 March 1912.

730. *The Passing of 'Miah* by D. P. Lucy. The Cork Dramatic Society, Dun Theatre, Cork: 10 (and possibly 11) April 1912.

731. *Struck* by Con O'Leary. Same theatre and location as above: 10 (and possibly 11) April 1912.

732. *The Hermit and the King* by Daniel Corkery. Same theatre and location as above: 10 (and possibly 11) April 1912.

733. *Patriots* by Lennox Robinson. The National Theatre Society Ltd., Abbey Theatre, Dublin: 11, 12, 13 April 1912.

734. *Hyacinth Halvey* by Lady Gregory. Same theatre and location as above: 11, 12, 13 April 1912.

735. *Judgment* by Joseph Campbell. Same theatre and location as above: 15 (and possibly 16) April 1912.

736. *Metempsychosis* by Thomas MacDonagh. Cliuthcheoiri na hEireann (Theatre of Ireland), Hardwicke Street Hall, Dublin: 18, 19, 20 April 1912.

737. *The Reformers* by Lewis Purcell. Same theatre and location as above: 18, 19, 20 April 1912.

738. *Riders to the Sea* by John Synge. The National Theatre Society Ltd., Abbey Theatre, Dublin: 18, 19, 20 April 1912.

739. *The Eloquent Dempsey* by William Boyle. Same theatre and location as above: 18, 19, 20 April 1912.

740. *In the Shadow of the Glen* by John Synge. Same theatre and location as above: 25, 26, 27 April 1912.

741. *The Man Who Missed the Tide* by W. F. Casey. Same theatre and location as above: 25, 26, 27 April 1912.

742. *Caitlin Ni hCallachain* by W. B. Yeats, translated by Father Kelly. Cliuthcheoiri na hEireann (Theatre of Ireland), Hardwicke Street Hall, Dublin: 2, 3, May 1912.

743. An Irish language play (title is not currently known) by Padraig O Seagda. Same theatre and location as above: 2, 3 May 1912.

744. *An Ri (The King)* by Padraic Pearse. St. Enda's School Theatre, St. Enda's School Rathfarnham, Co. Dublin: 15 June 1912.

745. *The Ordeal of David* by Victor O'D. Power. Cliuthcheoiri na hEireann (Theatre of Ireland), Hardwicke Street Hall, Dublin: 1 July 1912.

746. *Mixed Marriage* by St. John Ervine. The National Theatre Society Ltd., Abbey Theatre, Dublin: 26, 29 August 1912.

747. *The Rising of the Moon* by Lady Gregory. Same theatre and location as above: 26, 29 August 1912.

748. *Patriots* by Lennox Robinson. Same theatre and location as above: 27, 31 August 1912.

749. *The Workhouse Ward* by Lady Gregory and Douglas Hyde. Same theatre and location as above: 27, 31 August 1912.

750. *Kathleen Ni Houlihan* by W. B. Yeats. Same theatre and location as above: 28, 30, 31 August 1912.

751. *The Playboy of the Western World* by John Synge. Same theatre and location as above: 28, 30, 31 August 1912.

752. *Coats* by Lady Gregory. Same theatre and location as above: 12, 13, 14 September 1912.

753. *Maurice Harte* by T. C. Murray. Same theatre and location as above: 12, 13, 14 September 1912.

754. *The Rising of the Moon* by Lady Gregory. Same theatre and location as above: 12, 13, 14 September 1912.

755. *Riders to the Sea* by John Synge. Same theatre and location as above: 19, 20, 21 September 1912.

756. *The Eloquent Dempsey* by William Boyle. Same theatre and location as above: 19, 20, 21 September 1912.

757. *The Pie-dish* by George Fitzmaurice. Same theatre and location as above: 26, 27, 28 September 1912.

758. *The Countess Cathleen* by W. B. Yeats. Same theatre and location as above: 26, 27, 28 September 1912.

759. *Spreading the News* by Lady Gregory. Same theatre and location as above: 26, 27, 28 September 1912.

760. *Out of the Deep Shadow* by S. R. Day. The Independent Theatre Company, Gaiety Theater, Dublin: 30 September 1912.

761. *The Second Shepherd's Play* by Anon. The National Theatre Society Ltd. (probably the second company), Abbey Theatre, Dublin: 3, 4, 5 October 1912.

762. *The Country Dressmaker* by George Fitzmaurice. Same theatre and location as above: 3, 4, 5 October 1912.

763. *The Suburban Groove* by W. F. Casey. Same theatre and location as above: 10, 11, 12 October 1912.

764. *The Piper* by Norreys Connell. Same theatre and location as above: 10, 11, 12 October 1912.

765. *The Magnanimous Lover* by St. John Ervine. Same theatre and location as above: 17, 18, 19 October 1912.

766. *Family Failing* by William Boyle. Same theatre and location as above: 17, 18, 19 October 1912.

767. *In the Shadow of the Glen* by John Synge. The National Theatre Society Ltd., Abbey Theatre, Dublin: 24, 25, 26 October 1912.

768. *The White Cockade* by Lady Gregory. Same theatre and location as above: 24, 25, 26 October 1912.

769. *Thomas Muskerry* by Padraic Colum. Same theatre and location as above: 31 October and 1, 2 November 1912.

770. *The Glittering Gate* by Lord Dunsany. Same theatre and location as above: 31 October and 1, 2 November 1912.

771. *Patriots* by Lennox Robinson. Same theatre and location as above: 7, 8, 9 November 1912.

772. *Hyacinth Halvey* by Lady Gregory. Same theatre and location as above: 7, 8, 9 November 1912.

773. *A Pot of Broth* by W. B. Yeats. Same theatre and location as above: 14, 15, 16 November 1912.

774. *Maurice Harte* by T. C. Murray. Same theatre and location as above: 14, 15, 16 November 1912.

775. *The Rising of the Moon* by Lady Gregory. Same theatre and location as above: 14, 15, 16 November 1912.

776. *The Hour Glass* by W. B. Yeats. Same theatre and location as above: 21, 22, 23 November 1912.

777. *Damer's Gold* by Lady Gregory. Same theatre and location as above: 21, 22, 23 November 1912.

778. *Blind* by R. Cooney. Dramatic Society of the I. C. I. C. Y. M. A. (?), Greg Hall, South Mall, Cork: 21, 22 November 1912.

779. *Under Delusion* by Dixon Child. Same organization and location as above: 21, 22 November 1912.

780. *The Dream Market* by Bernard MacCarthy. Same organization and location as above: 21, 22 November 1912.

781. *Coats* by Lady Gregory. The National Theatre Society Ltd., Abbey Theatre, Dublin: 28, 29, 30 November 1912.

782. *Mixed Marriage* by St. John Ervine. Same theatre and location as above: 28, 29, 30 November 1912.

783. *Israel's Incense* by Daniel Corkery. The Cork Dramatic Society, the Cork Opera House, Cork: 2 December 1912.

784. *The Passing of 'Miah* by D. P. Lucy. Same theatre and location as above: 2 December 1912.

785. *The Onus of Ownership* by Daniel Corkery. Same theatre and location as above: 3 December 1912.

786. *The Crossing* by Con O'Leary. Same theatre and location as above: 3 December 1912.

787. *Drift* by John F. Lyons. Same theatre and location as above: 3 December 1912.

788. *Kathleen Ni Houlihan* by W. B. Yeats. The National Theatre Society Ltd., Abbey Theatre, Dublin: 3, 4, 5, 7 December 1912.

789. *Birthright* by T. C. Murray. Same theatre and location as above: 3, 4, 5, 7 December 1912.

790. *The Jackdaw* by Lady Gregory. Same theatre and location as above: 3, 4, 5, 7 December 1912.

791. *The Unicorn Under the Stars* by W. B. Yeats and Lady Gregory. Same theatre and location as above: 6, 7 December 1912.

792. *The Shewing Up of Blanco Posnet* by George Bernard Shaw. Same theatre and location as above: 6, 7 December 1912.

793. *Thompson in Tir na n'Og* by Gerald MacNamara. The Ulster Literary Theatre, Grand Opera House, Belfast: 9 December 1912.

794. *Family Rights* by M. F. Scott. Same theatre and location as above: 9 December 1912.

795. *Sweeping the County* by William Paul. Same theatre and location as above: 10 December 1912.

796. *The Gods at Play* by Mary Costello. A small company (?), Abbey Theatre, Dublin: 13 December 1912.

797. *A Little Christmas Miracle* by E. Hamilton Moore. The National Theatre Society Ltd., Abbey Theatre, Dublin: 26, 27, 28 December 1912.

798. *The Mineral Workers* by William Boyle. Same theatre and location, as above: 26, 27, 28 December 1912.

799. *Victims* by A. Patrick Wilson. The Irish Workers' Dramatic Club (usually the Irish Workers' Dramatic Company), Liberty Hall, Dublin: 26 December 1912.

1913

800. *The Return of Columbkille* by Father J. M. Costello. The Irish Historical Players, Ancient Order of Hibernians Hall, 31 Rutland Square, Dublin: 1 January 1913.

801. *The Building Fund* by William Boyle. The National Theatre Society Ltd., Abbey Theatre, Dublin: 2, 3, 4 January 1 1913.

    Another play most likely was offered on the same bill, but presently it is not known.

802. *The Return of Columbkille* by Father J. M. Costello. The Irish Historical Players, St. Francis Xavier Hall Dublin: 7 January 1913.

803. *Red Turf* by Rutherford Mayne. The National Theatre Society Ltd., Abbey Theatre, Dublin: 9, 10, 11 January 1913.

804. *The Country Dressmaker* by George Fitzmaurice. Same theatre and location as above: 9, 10, 11 January 1913.

805. *The Return of Columbkille* by Father J. M. Costello. The Irish Historical Players, Ancient Order of Hibernians Hall, Rutland Square, Dublin: 13 January 1913.

806. *Dervorgilla* by Lady Gregory. The National Theatre Society Ltd., Abbey Theatre, Dublin: 16, 17, 18 January 1913.

807. *Hyacinth Halvey* by Lady Gregory. Same theatre and location as above: 16, 17, 18 January 1913.

808. *Riders to the Sea* by John Synge. Same theatre and location as above: 16, 17, 18 January 1913.

809. *The Rising of the Moon* by Lady Gregory. Same theatre and location as above: 16, 17, 18 January 1913.

810. *The Dean of St. Patrick* by G. Sidney Paternoster. Same theatre and location as above: 23, 24, 25 January 1913. (This play was alone on its bill.)

811. *The Men in Possession* by J. Bernard MacCarthy. The Cork Dramatic Society, Dun Theatre, Cork: 29 (and possibly 30) January 1913.

812. *Wrecked* by J. Bernard MacCarthy. Same theatre and location as above: 29 (and possibly 30) January 1913.

813. The *Return of Columbkille* by Father J. M. Costello. The Irish Historical Players, Fr. Mathew Hall, Dublin: 31 January 1913.

814. *Sweeping the Country* by W. Paul. The Ulster Players (formerly the Ulster Literary Theatre), Abbey Theatre, Dublin: 31 January and 1 February 1913.

815. *Thompson in Tir na nOg* by Gerald MacNamara. Same theatre and location as above: 31 January and 1 February 1913.

816. *The Gaol Gate* by Lady Gregory. The National Theatre Society Ltd., Abbey Theatre, Dublin: 6, 7, 8 February 1913.

817. *The Casting Out of Martin Whelan* by R. J. Ray. Same theatre and location as above: 6, 7, 8 February 1913.

818. *Kathleen Ni Houlihan* by W. B. Yeats. Same theatre and location as above: 13, 14, 15 February 1913.

819. *Birthright* by T. C. Murray. Same theatre and location as above: 13, 14, 15 February 1913.

820. *The Workhouse Ward* by Lady Gregory and Douglas Hyde. Same theatre and location as above: 13, 14, 15 February 1913

821. *The Pot of Broth* by W. B. Yeats. Same theatre and location as above: 20, 21, 22 February 1913.

822. *Spreading the News* by Lady Gregory. Same theatre and location as above: 20, 21, 22 February 1913.

823. *Hannele* by Gerhardt Hauptmann. Same theatre and location as above: 20, 21, 22 February 1913.

824. *The Dean of St. Patrick's* by G. Sidney Paternoster. Same theatre and location as above: 27, 28 February and 1 March 1913.

825. *There are Crimes and Crimes* by August Strindberg. Same theatre and location as above: 6, 7, 8 March 1913.

826. *Riders to the Sea* by John Synge. Same theatre and location as above: 13, 14, 15 March 1913.

827. *The Cuckoo's Nest* by John Guinan. Same theatre and location as above: 13, 14, 15 March 1913.

828. *The Country Dressmaker* by George Fitzmaurice. Same theatre and location as above: 17 March 1913.

829. *An Tincear agus an tSidheog (The Tinker and the Sheeog)* by Douglas Hyde. Same theatre and location as above: 17 March 1913.

830. *The Rising of the Moon* by Lady Gregory. Same theatre and location as above: 22, 26 March 1913.

831. *The Cuckoo's Nest* by John Guinan. Same theatre and location as above: 22, 26 March 1913.

832. *Kathleen Ni Houlihan* by W. B. Yeats. Same theatre and location as above: 23, 25 March 1913.

833. *Birthright* by T. C. Murray. Same theatre and location as above: 23, 25 March 1913.

834. *The Workhouse Ward* by Lady Gregory and Douglas Hyde. Same theatre and location as above: 23, 25 March 1913.

835. *The Dean of St. Patrick's* by G. Sidney Paternoster. Same theatre and location as above: 24, 26 March 1913.

836. *Knocknagow* by R. G. Walsh. The Pioneer Dramatic Society, St. Francis Xavier Hall, Dublin: 24 March 1913.

837. *Hannele* by Gerhart Hauptmann. The National Theatre Society Ltd., Abbey Theatre, Dublin: 3, 4, 5 April 1913.

838. The *Building Fund* by William Boyle. Same theatre and location as above: 3, 4, 5 April 1913.

839. The *Home Coming* by Gertrude Robins. Same theatre and location as above: 10, 11, 12 April 1913.

840. *The Casting Out of Martin Whelan* by R. J. Ray. Same theatre and location as above: 10, 11, 12 April 1913.

841. The *Stranger* by August Strindberg. Same theatre and location as above: 17, 18, 19 April 1913.

842. *The Mineral Workers* by William Boyle. Same theatre and location as above: 17, 18, 19 April 1913.

843. *The Rising of the Moon* by Lady Gregory. Same theatre and location as above: 21, 23 April 1913.

844. *The Country Dressmaker* by George Fitzmaurice. Same theatre and location as above: 21, 23 April 1913.

845. *Kathleen Ni Houlihan* by W. B. Yeats. Same theatre and location as above: 22 April 1913.

846. *Birthright* by T. C. Murray. Same theatre and location as above: 22 April 1913.

847. *The Workhouse Ward* by Lady Gregory and Douglas Hyde. Same theatre and location as above: 22 April 1913.

848. *In the Shadow of the Glen* by John Synge. Same theatre and location as above: 24, 25, 26 April 1913.

849. *Broken Faith* by S. R. Day and G. D. Cummings. Same theatre and location as above: 24, 25, 26 April 1913.

850. *The Magic Glasses* by George Fitzmaurice. Same theatre and location as above: 24, 25, 26 April 1913.

851. *Bairbre Ruadh* by Padraic O'Conaire. A Gaelic League Branch, Abbey Theatre: 2, 3, May 1913.

852. *Mac na Mna Deirce* Irish translation by Michael MacRury and Sean MacGiollarna of Seumas O'Kelly's The S*huiler's Child.* Same organization and location as above: 2, 3 May 1913.

853. *An Docthuir (The Doctor)* by Seumas O'Beirne. The Croke Gaelic Club, Colmcill Hall, Blackhall Street, Dublin: 4 May 1913.

854. *The Land of Heart's Desire* by W. B. Yeats. The National Theatre Society Ltd., Abbey Theatre, Dublin: 9 May 1913.

855. *Patriots* by Lennox Robinson. Same theatre and location as above: 9 May 1913.

856. *The Magnanimous Lover* by St. John Ervine. Same theatre and location as above: 9 May 1913.

857. *Maurice Harte* by T. C. Murray. Same theatre and location as above: 9 May 1913.

858. *The Rising of the Moon* by Lady Gregory. Same theatre and location as above: 9 May 1913.

859. *The Devil's Disciple* by Bernard Shaw. The Repertory Theatre (formerly the Independent Theatre Company), Gaiety Theatre, Dublin: 12, 13, 14, 15, 16, 17 May 1913.

860. *The Post Office* by Rabindranath Tagore. The National Theatre Society Ltd., Abbey Theatre, Dublin: 17 May 1913.

861. *An Ri (The King) by* Padraic Pearse. St. Enda's School Theatre, Abbey Theatre, Dublin: 17 May 1913.

862. *Casadh an tSugain (The Twisting of the Rope)* by Douglas Hyde. The Gaelic Branch of the Five Provinces, Molesworth Hall Dublin: 31 May 1913.

863. An Irish language play (title is not currently known) by (?) Same organization and location as above: 31 May 1913.

864. *An Ri (The King)* by Padraic Pearse. St. Enda's School Theatre, open-air on the grounds of St. Enda's School, County Dublin: 14 June 1913.

865. "A Short play dealing with '98," title and author unknown, was performed by the Fianna Players of the Fianna Eireann, under Constance Markievicz, open-air on the grounds of St. Enda's School, County Dublin: 15 June 1913.

866. *Riders to Sea* by John Synge. The National Theatre Society Ltd., Abbey Theatre, Dublin: 25, 28 August 1913.

867. *Damer's Gold* by Lady Gregory. Same theatre and location as above: 25, 28 August 1913.

868. *Spreading the News* by Lady Gregory. Same theatre and location as above: 25, 28 August 1913.

869. *In the Shadow of the Glen* by John Synge. Same theatre and location as above: 26, 30 August 1913.

870. *The Mineral Workers* by William Boyle. Same theatre and location as above: 26, 30 August 1913.

871. The *Playboy of the Western World* by John Synge. Same theatre and location as above: 27, 30 August 1913.

872. *The Rising of the Moon* by Lady Gregory. Same theatre and location as above: 27, 30 August 1913.

873. *The Magnanimous Lover* by St. John Ervine. Same theatre and location as above: 4, 5, 6 September 1913.

874. *The Cuckoo's Nest* by John Guinan. Same theatre and location as above: 4, 5, 6 September 1913.

875. *Sovereign Love* by T. C. Murray. Same theatre and location as above: 11, 12, 13 September 1913.

876. *The Casting Out of Martin Whelan* by R. J. Ray. Same theatre and location as above: 11, 12, 13 September 1913.

877. *The Marriage* by Douglas Hyde. Same theatre and location as above: 18, 19, 20 September 1913.

878. *The Country Dressmaker* by George Fitzmaurice. Same theatre and location as above: 18, 19, 20 September 1913.

879. The *Gaol Gate* by Lady Gregory. Same theatre and location as above: 25, 26, 27 September 1913.

880. *Family Failing* by William Boyle. Same theatre and location as above: 25, 26, 27 September 1913.

881. *The Post Office* by Rabindranath Tagore. Same theatre and location as above: 2, 3, 4 October 1913.

882. *The Mine Land* by Joseph Connolly. Same theatre and location as above: 2, 3, 4 October 1913.

883. *Toilers* by S. R. Day. The Irishwomen's Reform League, Sackville Hall Dublin: 6 October 1913.

884. *Hannele* by Gerhardt Hauptmann. The National Theatre Society Ltd., Abbey Theatre, Dublin: 9, 10, 11 October 1913.

885. *The Building Fund* by William Boyle. Same theatre and location as above: 9, 10, 11 October 1913.

886. *The White Cockade* by Lady Gregory. Same theatre and location as above: 13, 14, 15 October 1913.

887. *The Piper* by Norreys Connell. Same theatre and location as above: 13, 14, 15 October 1913.

888. *My Lord* by Mrs. Bart Kennedy. Same theatre and location as above: 16, 17, 18 October 1913.

889. *Patriots* by Lennox Robinson. Same theatre and location as above: 16, 17, 18 October 1913.

890. *The Dean of St. Patrick's* by G. Sidney Paternoster. Same theatre and location as above: 16, 17, 18 October 1913.

891. *Kathleen Ni Houlihan* by W. B. Yeats. Same theatre and location as above: 23, 24, 25 October 1913.

892. *The Canavans* by Lady Gregory. Same theatre and location as above: 23, 24, 25 October 1913.

893. *The Second Shepherd's Play* by Anon. Same theatre and location as above: 27, 28, 29 October 1913.

894. *Broken Faith* by S. R. Day and G. D. Cummins. Same theatre and location as above: 27, 28, 29 October 1913.

895. *The Magic Glasses* by George Fitzmaurice. Same theatre and location as above: 27, 28, 29 October 1913.

896. *The King's Threshold by* W. B. Yeats. Same theatre and location as above: 30, 31 October and 1 November 1913.

897. *Damer's Gold* by Lady Gregory. Same theatre and location as above: 30, 31 October and 1 November 1913.

898. *Riders to the Sea* by John Synge. Same theatre and location as above: 6, 7, 8 November 1913.

899. *The Eloquent Dempsey* by William Boyle. Same theatre and location as above: 6, 7, 8 November 1913.

900. *The Gombeen Man* by R. J. Ray. Same theatre and location as above: 11, 12 November 1913.

901. *Spreading the News* by Lady Gregory. Same theatre and location as above: 11, 12 November 1913.

902. *The Suburban Groove* by W. F. Casey. Same theatre and location as above: 13, 14, 15 November 1913.

903. *The Rising of the Moon* by Lady Gregory. Same theatre and location as above: 13, 14, 15 November 1913.

904. *Sovereign Love* by T. C. Murray. Same theatre and location as above: 18, 19 November 1913.

905. *Birthright* by T. C. Murray. Same theatre and location as above: 18, 19 November 1913.

906. *Hyacinth Halvey* by Lady Gregory. Same theatre and location as above: 18, 19 November 1913.

907. *The Critics, or a New Play at the Abbey* by St. John Ervine. Same theatre and location as above: 20, 21, 22 November 1913.

908. *Mixed Marriage* by St. John Ervine. Same theatre and location as above: 20, 21, 22 November 1913.

909. *Love and Land* by Lynn Doyle. The Ulster Theatre (formerly the Ulster Players and the Ulster Literary Theatre), Grand Opera House, Belfast: 24 November 1913.

910. *If* by Rutherford Mayne. Same theatre and location as above: 25 November 1913.

911. *Caitlin Ni hCallachain* by W. B. Yeats, translated by Father O'Kelly. Same theater as above: 26, 28 November 1913.

912. An Irish language play (title is not currently known) by (?). Same organization and location as above: 26, 28 November 1913.

913. There was a theatrical presentation at St. Enda's School Theatre, County Dublin: 1 December 1913.

914. *The Mine Land* by Joseph Connolly. The National Theatre Society Ltd., Abbey Theatre, Dublin: 2, 3 December 1913.

915. *The Piper* by Norreys Connell. Same theatre and location as above: 2, 3 December 1913.

916. *The Man Who Missed the Tide* by W. F. Casey. Same theatre and location as above: 4, 5, 6 December 1913.

917. *The Workhouse Ward* by Lady Gregory and Douglas Hyde. Same theatre and location as above: 4, 5, 6 December 1913.

918. *In the Shadow of the Glen* by John Synge. Same theatre and location as above: 9, 10 December 1913.

919. *Patriots* by Lennox Robinson. Same theatre and location as above: 9, 10 December 1913.

920. *MacDaragh's Wife* by Lady Gregory. Same theatre and location as above: 11, 12, 13 December 1913.

921. *The Mineral Workers* by William Boyle. Same theatre and location as above: 11, 12, 13 December 1913.

922. *Duty* by Seumas O'Brien. Same theatre and location as above: 16, 17 December 1913.

923. *The Gaol Gate* by Lady Gregory. Same theatre and location as above: 16, 17 December 1913.

924. *The Building Fund* by William Boyle. Same theatre and location as above: 16, 17 December 1913.

925. *The Bribe* by Seumas O'Kelly. Same theatre and location as above: 18, 19, 20 December 1913.

926. *The Critics, or a New Play at the Abbey* by St. John Ervine. Same theatre and location as above: 18, 19, 20 December 1913.

927. *Duty* by Seumas O'Brien. Same theatre and location as above: 26, 27 December 1913.

928. *The Eloquent Dempsey* by William Boyle. Same location as above: 26, 27 December 1913.

929. *Coats* by Lady Gregory. Same theatre and location as above: 29, 30, 31 December 1913.

930. *Mixed Marriage* by St. John Ervine. Same theatre and location as above: 29, 30, 31 December 1913.

931. *Family Failing* by William Boyle. Same theatre and location as above: 31 December 1913.

932. At least one Gaelic language play was performed (probably by a Gaelic League Branch theatre), 31 December 1913. Specific title, author, organization, and location are unknown.

1914

933. *Kathleen Ni Houlihan* by W. B. Yeats. The National Theatre Society Ltd., Abbey Theatre, Dublin: 1, 2, 3 January 1914.

934. *Family Failing* by William Boyle. Same theatre and location as above: 1, 2, 3 January 1914.

935. *The Gombeen Man* by R. J. Ray. Same theatre and location as above: 13, 14 January 1914.

936. *The Workhouse Ward* by Lady Gregory and Douglas Hyde. Same theatre and location as above: 13, 14 January 1914.

937. *The Clancy Name* by Lennox Robinson. Same theatre and location as above: 15, 16, 17 January 1914.

938. *The Country Dressmaker* by George Fitzmaurice. Same theatre and location as above: 15, 16, 17 January 1914.

939. *The Bribe* by Seumas O'Kelly. Same theatre and location as above: 20, 21 January 1914.

940. *The Sovereign Love* by T. C. Murray. Same theatre and location as above: 20, 21 January 1914.

941. *The King's Threshold* by W. B. Yeats. Same theatre and location as above: 22, 23, 24 January 1914.

942. *The Well of Saints* by John Synge. Same theatre and location as above: 22, 23, 24 January 1914.

943. An Irish language play (title is not currently known) by (?) A Gaelic League Branch, Gaelic League Hall, Dublin: 24 January 1914.

944. An Irish language play (title is not currently known) by Piaras Beaslai. Same organization and location as above: 24 January 1914.

945. *The Canavans* by Lady Gregory. The National Theatre Society Ltd., Abbey Theatre, Dublin: 27, 28 January 1914.

946. *The Shewing Up of Blanco Posnet* by George Bernard Shaw. Same theatre and location as above: 27, 28 January 1914.

947. *David Mahony* by Victor O'D. Power. Same theatre and location as above: 27, 28 January 1914.

948. *The Jackdaw* by Lady Gregory. Same theatre and location as above: 27, 28 January 1914.

949. *Kathleen Ni Houlihan* by W. B. Yeats. Same theatre and location as above: 27, 28 January 1914.

950. *The Dawn of Common Sense* by (?) The Colmcille Branch of the Gaelic League, Father Mathew Hall Dublin: 30 January 1914.

951. At least one short play in Irish was premiered by a Gaelic League Branch at the Mansion House, Dublin: 13 February 1914.

952. *Maistin an Bhearla (The Mastiff of the English Language)* by Douglas Hyde. The Irish Players, Abbey Theatre, Dublin: 19 February 1914.

953. An Irish language play (title is not currently known) by ? Same organization and location as above: 19 February 1914.

954. An Irish language play (title is not currently known) by (?). Same organization and location as above: 19 February 1914.

955. *Matchmakers* by Seumas O'Kelly. The Croke Club, Foresters Hall, 41 Parnell Square (formerly Rutland Square), Dublin: 1 March 1914.

956. *An Doctuir (The Doctor)* by Seumas O'Beirne. Same organization and location as above: 1 March 1914.

957. *Evening* by Rutherford Mayne. The Ulster Theatre (formerly the Ulster Players), Grand Opera House, Belfast: 2 (and possibly additional dates and plays to 7) March 1914.

958. *Kathleen Ni Houlihan* by W. B. Yeats. The Davis Players, Rotunda Hall, Dublin: 4 March 1914.

959. *The Orangeman* by St. John Ervine. The National Theatre Society Ltd., Abbey Theatre, Dublin: 13, 14, 17, 19, 20, 21 March 1914.

960. *The Lord Mayor* by Edward McNulty. Same theatre and location as above: 13, 14, 17, 19, 20, 21 March 1914.

961. *The Rising of the Moon* by Lady Gregory. Same theatre and organization as above: 17 March 1914.

962. *Love and Land* by Lynn Doyle. The Ulster Theatre, Grand Opera House, Belfast: 19 March 1914.

963. *The Enthusiast* by Lewis Purcell. Same theatre and location as above: 19 March 1914.

964. *The Drone* by Rutherford Mayne. Same theatre and location as above: 20, 21 March 1914.

965. *The Turn of the Road* by Rutherford Mayne. Same theatre and organization as above: 21 March 1914.

966. *A Question of Honor* by Annie J. W. Lloyd. Ladies Committee of Feis Ceoil, Abbey Theatre, Dublin: 25 March 1914.

In his list of premieres, Robert Hogan incorrectly dates this production and the next, O'Brien's *Candidates*, as 27 March (Hogan, Burnham and Poteet 467).

967. *Candidates* by Cruise O'Brien. Same organization and location as above: 25 March 1914.

968. *Kinship* by J. Bernard MacCarthy. The National Theatre Society Ltd., Abbey Theatre, Dublin: 2, 3, 4 April 1914.

969. *Mirandolina* by Carlo Goldini translated by Lady Gregory. Same theatre and location as above: 2, 3, 4 April 1914.

970. *Hyacinth Halvey* by Lady Gregory. Same theatre and location as above: 2, 3, 4 April 1914.

971. *The Orangeman* by St. John Ervine. Same theatre and location as above: 13, 17 April 1914.

972. *Mirandolina* by Carlo Goldini translated by Lady Gregory. Same theatre and location as above: 22, 24 April 1914.

973. *Hyacinth Halvey* by Lady Gregory. Same theatre and location as above: 22, 24 April 1914.

974. *The Cobbler* by A. Patrick Wilson. Same theatre and location as above: 13, 15, 18, 21, 23, 25 April 1914.

975. *The Lord Mayor* by Edward McNulty. Same theatre and location as above: 21, 23, 25 April 1914.

976. *Kincora* by Lady Gregory. Same theatre and location as above: 14, 16, 18, 20, 25 April 1914.

977. *Spreading the News* by Lady Gregory. Same theatre and location as above: 20, 25 April 1914.

978. *The Prodigal Daughter* by Francis Sheehy-Skeffington. The Irish Woman's Franchise League, Molesworth Hall, Dublin: 24 April 1914.

979. An Irish language play (title is not currently known) by Miss Dowling. Gaelic Class Students, Marlboro Street School, Father Mathew Hall, Dublin: 1 May 1914.

980. *Love and Land* by Lynn Doyle. The Ulster Theatre, Abbey Theatre, Dublin: 1, 2 May 1914.

981. *The Mist That Does Be on the Bog* by Gerald MacNamara. Same theatre and location as above: 1, 2 May 1914.

982. *The True Born Irishman* by Charles Macklin. Performed by actors formerly of the Theatre of Ireland, a benefit for the Sacred Heart Orphanage, Abbey Theatre, Dublin: 12, 13 May 1914.

983. *How He Lied to Her Husband* by Bernard Shaw. Same organization and location as above: 12, 13 May 1914.

984. *Her Second Chance* by H. B. O'Hanlon, St, Mary's College Literary and Dramatic Society of Rathmines, Abbey Theatre, Dublin: 19 May 1914.

985. *Posadh an Iasgaine (Marriage of Iasgaine)* by Sean O Murthuile, A Gaelic League Branch, Gaelic League Hall, Dublin: 20 June 1914.

986. *Cluiche Cartai (The Card Game)* by (?). Same organization and location as above: 20 June 1914.

987. *The Bribe* by Seumas O'Kelly. The National Theatre Society Ltd., Abbey Theatre, Dublin: 27, 28, 29 August 1914.

988. *A Minute's Wait* by Martin J. McHugh. Same theatre and location as above: 27, 28, 29 August 1914.

989. *The Supplanter* by J. Bernard MacCarthy. Same theatre and location as above: 3, 4, 5 September 1914.

990. *Duty* by Seumas O'Brien. Same theatre and location as above: 3, 4, 5 September 1914.

991. *The Dark Hour* by R. A. Christie. Same theatre and location as above: 9, 10, 11, 12 September 1914.

992. *The Suburban Groove* by W. F. Casey. Same theatre and location as above: 9, 10, 11, 12 September 1914.

993. *The Cobbler* by A. Patrick Wilson. Same theatre and location as above: 16, 17, 18, 19 September 1914.

994. *Marurice Harte* by T. C. Murray. Same theatre and location as above: 16, 17, 18, 19 September 1914.

995. *Sovereign Love* by T. C. Murray. Same theatre and location as above: 16, 17, 18, 19 September 1914.

996. *The Crossing* by Con O'Leary. Same theatre and location as above: 23, 24, 25, 26 September 1914.

997. *The Eloquent Dempsey* by William Boyle. Same theatre and location as above: 23, 24, 25, 26 September 1914.

998. *The Dark Hour* by R. A. Christie. Same theatre and location as above: 30 September and 1, 2, 3 October 1914.

999. *The Prodigal* by Walter Riddall. Same theatre and location as above: 30 September and 1, 2, 3 October 1914.

1000. *The Man Who Missed the Tide* by W. F. Casey. Same theatre and location as above: 6, 7, 8, 9, 10 October 1914.

1001. *A Minute's Wait* by Martin J. McHugh. Same theatre and location as above: 6, 7, 8, 9, 10 October 1914.

1002. *The Cobweb* by F. Jay. Same theatre and location as above: 13, 14, 15, 16, 17 October 1914.

1003. *The Mineral Workers* by William Boyle. Same theatre and location as above: 13, 14, 15, 16, 17 October 1914.

1004. *The Jug of Sorrow* by W. P. Ryan. Same theatre and location as above: 20, 21, 22, 23, 24 October 1914.

1005. *The Country Dressmaker* by George Fitzmaurice. Same theatre and location as above: 20, 21, 22, 23, 24 October 1914.

1006. *Birthright* by T. C. Murray. Same theatre and location as above: 27, 28, 29, 30, 31 October 1914.

1007. *The Building Fund* by William Boyle. Same theatre and organization as above: 27, 28, 29, 30, 31 October 1914.

1008. *The Dream Physician* by Edward Martyn. The Irish Theatre Company, Little Theatre, 40 Upper O'Connell Street, Dublin: 2, 3, 4, 5, 6, 7 November 1914.

1009. *The Slough* by A. Patrick Wilson. The National Theatre Society Ltd., Abbey Theatre, Dublin: 3, 4, 5, 6, 7 November 1914.

1010. *The Rising of the Moon* by Lady Gregory. Same theatre and location as above: 3, 4, 5, 6, 7 November 1914.

1011. *The Bribe* by Seumas O'Kelly. Same theatre and location as above: 10, 11, 12, 13, 14 November 1914.

1012. *Duty* by Seumas O'Brien. Same theatre and location as above: 10, 11, 12, 13, 14 November 1914.

1013. *The Slough* by A. Patrick Wilson. Same theatre and location as above: 17, 18, 19, 20, 21 November 1914.

1014. *A Minute's Wait* by Martin J. McHugh. Same theatre and location as above: 17, 18, 19, 20, 21 November 1914.

1015. *The Jug of Sorrow* by W. P. Ryan. Same theater and location as above: 24, 25, 26, 27, 28 November 1914.

1016. *Maurice Harte* by T. C. Murray. Same theatre and location as above: 24, 25, 26, 27, 28 November 1914.

1017. *The Shewing Up of Blanco Posnet* by George Bernard Shaw. Same theatre and location as above: 24, 25, 26, 27, 28 November 1914.

1018. *Family Failing* by William Boyle. Same theatre and location as above: 30 November and 1, 2 December 1914.

1019. *Hyacinth Halvey* by Lady Gregory. Same theatre and location as above: 30 November and 1, 2, December.

1020. *The Cobwebs* by F. Jay. Same theatre and location as above: 3, 4, 5 December 1914.

1021. *The Suburban Groove* by W. F. Casey. Same theatre and location as above: 3, 4, 5 December 1914.

1022. *If* by Rutherford Mayne. The Ulster Theatre, Gaiety Theatre, Dublin: 16, 17, 19 December 1914.

1023. *The Drone* by Rutherford Mayne. Same theatre and location as above: 16, 17, 19 December 1914.

1024. *Thompson in Tir na nOg* by Gerald MacNamara. Same theatre and location as above: 16, 17, 19 December 1914.

1025. *Kathleen Ni Houlihan* by W. B. Yeats. The National Theatre Society Ltd., Abbey Theatre, Dublin: 26, 28, 29, 30, 31 December 1914.

1026. *The Critic* by Richard Brinsley Sheridan. Same theatre and location as above: 26, 28, 29 30, 31 December 1914.

1915

1027. *Kathleen Ni Houlihan* by W. B. Yeats. The National Theatre Society Ltd., Abbey Theatre, Dublin: 1, 2 January 1915.

1028. *The Critic* by Richard Brinsley Sheridan. Same theatre and location as above: 1, 2 January 1915.

1029. *The Troth* by Rutherford Mayne, translated into Irish by Liam O'Domhnaill. The Irish Theatre Company, Hardwicke Street Hall, Dublin: 4, 5, 6, 7, 8, 9 January 1915.

1030. *The Revolt* by Villers de l'Isle Adam. Same theatre and location as above: 4, 5, 6, 7, 8, 9 January 1915.

1031. *The Swan Song* by Anton Tchekoff (translated by Marian Fell). Same theatre and location as above: 4, 5, 6, 7, 8, 9 January 1915.

1032. *The Phoenix on the Roof* by Eimar O'Duffy. Same theatre and location as above: 4, 5, 6, 7, 8, 9 January 1915.

1033. *Patriots* by Lennox Robinson. The National Theatre Society Ltd., Abbey Theatre, Dublin: 6, 7, 8, 9 January 1915.

1034. *The Workhouse Ward* by Lady Gregory and Douglas Hyde. Same theatre and location as above: 6, 7, 8, 9 January 1914.

1035. *The Casting Out of Martin Whelan* by R. J. Ray. Same theatre and location as above: 20, 21, 22, 23 January 1915.

1036. *Sovereign Love* by T. C. Murray. Same theatre and location as above: 20, 21, 22, 23 January 1914.

1037. *By Word of Mouth* by F. C. Moore and W. P. Flannagan. Same theatre and location as above: 27, 28, 29, 30 January 1915.

1038. *Mixed Marriage* by St. John Ervine. Same theatre and location as above: 27, 28, 29, 30 January 1915.

1039. *The Spoiled Buddha* by Helen Waddell. The Ulster Theatre, Grand Opera House, Belfast: 1 (and possibly more dates) February 1915.

1040. *Snowdrop Jane* by Shan F. Bullock. Same theatre and location as above: 2 (and possibly more dates) February 1915.

1041. *The Magnanimous Lover* by St. John Ervine. The National Theatre Society Ltd., Abbey Theatre, Dublin: 3, 4, 5, 6 February 1915.

1042. *The Country Dressmaker* by George Fitzmaurice. Same theatre and location as above: 3, 4, 5, 6 February 1915.

1043. *The Dreamers* by Lennox Robinson. Same theatre and location as above: 10, 11, 12, 13 February 1915.

1044. *The Dream Physician* by Edward Martyn. The Irish Theatre Company, Hardwicke Street Hall, Dublin: 12, 13, 15, 16 February 1915.

1045. *In the Shadow of the Glen* by John Synge. The National Theatre Society Ltd., Abbey Theatre, Dublin: 18, 19, 20, February 1915.

1046. *The Eloquent Dempsey* by William Boyle. Same theatre and location as above: 18, 19, 20 February 1915.

1047. *The Slough* by A. Patrick Wilson. Same theatre and location as above: 24, 25, 26, 27 February 1915.

1048. *The Jackdaw* by Lady Gregory. Same theatre and location as above: 24, 25, 26, 27 February 1915.

1049. *The Man Who Missed the Tide* by W. F. Casey. Same theatre and location as above: 3, 4, 5, 6 March 1915.

1050. *Spreading the News* by Lady Gregory. Same theatre and location as above: 3, 4, 5 March 1915.

1051. At least one play was presented for the Robert Emmet Anniversary celebration, Rotunda Hall, Dublin: 4 March 1915. Title and theatre/organization is not currently known.

1052. *Family Failing* by William Boyle. The National Theatre Society Ltd., Abbey Theatre, Dublin: 10, 11, 12, 13 March 1915.

1053. *A Minute's Wait* by Martin J. McHugh. Same theatre and location as above: 10, 11,12,13 March 1915.

1054. *The Suburban Groove* by W. F. Casey. Same theatre and organization as above: 17, 18, 19, 20 March 1915.

1055. *Duty* by Seumas O'Brien. Same theatre and location as above: 17, 18, 19, 20 March 1915.

1056. *The Green Helmet* by W. B. Yeats. Same theatre and location as above: 24, 25, 26, 27 March 1915.

1057. *The Mineral Workers* by William Boyle. Same theatre and location as above: 24, 25, 26, 27 March 1915.

1058. *The Bargain* by William Crone. Same theatre and location as above: 5, 6, 7 April 1915.

1059. *The Philosopher* by Martin J. McHugh. Same theatre and location as above: 5, 6, 7 April 1915.

1060. *Shanwalla* by Lady Gregory. Same theatre and location as above: 8, 9, 10 April 1915.

1061. *Sovereign Love* by T. C. Murray. Same theatre and location as above: 8, 9, 10 April 1915.

1062. *The Walls of Athens* by Eimar O'Duffy. The Irish Theatre Company, Hardwicke Street Hall, Dublin: 19, 20, 21, 22, 23, 24 April 1915.

1063. *Pagans* by Thomas MacDonagh. Same theatre and location as above: 19, 20, 21, 22, 23, 24 April 1915.

1064. *Knocknagow* by R. G. Walsh. Theatre/organization Unknown, benefit for the nurses of the poor, Abbey Theatre, Dublin: 23, 24 April 1915.

1065. *Maurice Harte* by T. C. Murray. The National Theatre Society Ltd., Abbey Theatre, Dublin: 26 April 1915.

1066. *The Shewing Up of Blanco Posnet* by George Bernard Shaw. Same theatre and location as above: 26, 27, 30 April 1915.

1067. *The Building Fund* by William Boyle. Same theatre and location as above: 27, 30 April 1915.

1068. *The Magnanimous Lover* by St. John Ervine. Same theatre and location as above: 28, April and 1 May 1915.

1069. *The Eloquent Dempsey* by William Boyle. Same theatre and location as above: 28 April and 1 May 1915.

1070. *Riders to the Sea* by John Synge. Same theatre and location as above: 29 April and 1 May 1915.

1071. *The Playboy of the Western World* by John Synge. Same theatre and location as above: 29 April and 1 May 1915.

1072. *The Clancy Name* by Lennox Robinson. Same theatre and location as above: 5, 6, 7 May 1915.

1073. *The Lord Mayor* by Edward McNulty. Same theatre and location as above: 5, 6, 7 May 1915.

1074. *Iosagan* by Padraic Pearse. St. Enda's School Theatre and the Irish Theatre Company, Hardwick Street Hall Dublin: 20, 22, May 1915.

1075. *The Master* by Padraic Pearse. Same theatre(s) and location as above: 20, 22 May 1915.

1076. *Casadh an tSugain (The Twisting of the Rope)* by Douglas Hyde. The Irish Theatre Company, Hardwicke Street Hall, Dublin: 29 May 1915.

1077. *An tSnaidhm (The Knot)* by A. Labhraidh. Same theatre and location as above: 29 May 1915.

1078. *Uncle Vanya* by Anton Tchekoff. The Irish Theatre Company, Hardwicke Street Theatre, Dublin: 28, 29, 30 June and 1, 2, 3 July 1915.

1079. At least one play was presented at the Oireachtas 1915, title and organization is not known, Dundalk: 25, 30 July 1915.

1080. *The Lad from Largymore* by Seumas MacManus. Performed by Irish Theatre Company actors, St. Enda's School, County Dublin: 5 September 1915.

1081. At least one play was presented by the Irish Workers' Dramatic Company, Liberty Hall, Dublin: 19 September 1915.

1082. One or two plays were presented by an unknown company (most likely actors from the Irish Theatre Company since two of the company's directors were Thomas MacDonagh and Joseph Plunkett), benefit for the Equipment Fund of the Irish Volunteers, Hall, 41 Parnell Square, Dublin: 17 October 1915.

1083. An Irish language play (title is not currently known) by Piarais Beaslai. A Gaelic League Branch, Abbey Theatre, Dublin: 2 November 1915.

1084. *An tSnaidhm (The Knot)* by A. Labhraidh. Same organization and location as above: 2 November 1915.

1085. *Irish Dramatic Tableaux..* Company unknown, Abbey Theatre, Dublin: 3 November 1915.

1086. *The Recruiting Officer* by George Farquhar. Irish Women's Workers' Union, Liberty Hall, Dublin: 7 November 1915.

1087. *The Privilege of Place* by Edward Martyn. The Irish Theatre Company, Hardwicke Street Hall, Dublin: 8, 9, 10, 11, 12, 13 November 1915.

1088. *Maurice Harte* by T. C. Murray. The National Theatre Society Ltd., Abbey Theatre, Dublin: 10, 11, 12, 13 November 1915.

1089. *Sovereign Love* by T. C. Murray. Same theatre and location as above: 10, 11, 12, 13 November 1915.

1090. *The Eloquent Dempsey* by William Boyle. The Irish Workers' Dramatic Company, Liberty Hall, Dublin: 21 November 1915.

1091. *The Eloquent Dempsey* by William Boyle. The National Theatre Society Ltd., Abbey Theatre, Dublin: 23, 24, 25, 26, 27 November 1915.

1092. *In the Shadow of the Glen* by John Synge. Same theatre and location as above: 23, 24, 25, 26, 27 November 1915.

1093. *An Exile of Erin* by Thomas Finnigan. The Brinsley Sheridan Players, Hardwicke Street Theatre, Dublin: 24, 25 November 1915.

1094. *John Ferguson* by St. John Ervine. The National Theatre Society Ltd., Abbey Theatre, Dublin: 30 November and 1, 2, 3, 4 December 1915.

1095. *Patriots* by Lennox Robinson. Same theatre and location as above: 7, 8, 9, 10, 11 December 1915.

1096. *Duty* by Seumas O'Brien. Same theatre and location as above: 7, 8, 9, 10, 11 December 1915.

1097. *The Drone* by Rutherford Mayne. The Ulster Theatre, Gaiety Theatre, Dublin: 14, 15, 16, 17, 18 December 1915.

1098. *Thompson in Tir na nOg* by Gerald MacNamara. Same theatre and location as above: 14, 15, 16, 17, 18 December 1915.

1099. *The Matchmakers* by Seumas O'Kelly. The Irish Workers' Dramatic Company, Liberty Hall, Dublin: 19, 20 December 1915.

1100. An Irish language play (title is not currently known) by Piarais Beaslai. A Gaelic League Branch, Rotunda Hall Dublin: 20 December 1915.

1101. *A May Eve in Stephen's Green* an operetta by Lily M. O'Brennan. Same organization and location as above: 20 December 1915.

1102. *The Building Fund* by William Boyle. The Irish Workers' Dramatic Company, Liberty Hall, Dublin: 26 December 1915.

1103. *The Lord Mayor* by Edward McNulty. The National Theatre Society Ltd., Abbey Theatre, Dublin: 27, 28, 29, 30, 31 December 1915.

1104. *A Minute's Wait* by Martin J. McHugh. Same theatre and location as above: 27, 28, 29, 30, 31 December 1915.

1105. One play was presented by the Irish Workers' Dramatic Company, Liberty Hall, Dublin: 27, 28 December 1915.

1106. *The Swan Song* by Anton Tchekoff. The Irish Theatre Company, Hardwicke Street Hall, Dublin: 27, 28, 29, 30, 31 December 1915.

1107. *The Phoenix on the Roof* by Eimar O'Duffy. Same theatre and location as above: 27, 28, 29, 30, 31 December 1915.

1108. *Bairbre Ruadh* by Padraic O Canaire. Same theatre and location as above: 27, 28, 29, 30, 31 December 1915.

1109. *Author! Author!* by John MacDonagh. Same theatre and location as above: 27, 28, 29, 30, 31 December 1915.

1916

1110. *The Lord Mayor* by Edward McNulty. The National Theatre Society Ltd., Abbey Theatre, Dublin: 1 January 1916.

1111. *A Minute's Wait* by Edward J. McHugh. Same theatre and location as above: 1 January 1916.

1112. *The Swan Song* by Anton Tchekoff. The Irish Theatre Company, Hardwick Street Hall, Dublin: 1 January 1916.

1113. *The Phoenix on the Roof* by Eimar O'Duffy. Same theatre and location as above: 1 January 1916.

1114. *Bairbha Ruadh* by Padraic O Canaire. Same theatre and location as above: 1 January 1916.

1115. *Author! Author!* by John MacDonagh. Same theater and location as above: 1 January 1916.

1116. *Fraternity* by Bernard Duffy. The National Theatre Society Ltd., Abbey Theatre, Dublin: 4, 5, 6, 7, 8 January 1916.

1117. *The Suburban Groove* by W. F. Casey. Same theatre and location as above: 4, 5, 6, 7, 8 January 1916.

1118. *The Bishop's Candlestick* by (?) The Irish Workers' Dramatic Company, Liberty Hall, Dublin: 9 January 1916.

1119. *The Lad from Largymore* by Seumas MacManus. Same theatre and location as above: 9 January 1916.

1120. *Fraternity* by Bernard Duffy. The National Theatre Society Ltd., Abbey Theatre, Dublin: 11, 12, 13, 14, 15 January 1916.

1121. *The Prodigal* by Walter Riddall. Same theatre and location as above: 11, 12, 13, 14, 15 January 1916.

1122. *Leadin' Road to Donegal* by Seumas MacManus. The Irish Workers' Dramatic Company, Liberty Hall Dublin: 16 January 1916.

1123. *The Mineral Workers* by William Boyle. The National Theatre Society Ltd., Abbey Theatre, Dublin: 25, 26, 27, 28, 29 January 1916.

1124. *Spreading the News* by Lady Gregory. Same theatre and location as above: 25, 26, 27, 28, 29 January 1916.

1125. *Roisin's Robe* by P. Hogan. Same theatre and location as above: 30 January 1916.

1126. *The Matchmakers* by Seumas O'Kelly. Same theatre and location as above: 30 January 1916.

1127. *The Bribe* by Seumas O'Kelly. The National Theatre Society Ltd., Abbey Theatre, Dublin: 1, 2, 3, 4, 5 February 1916.

1128. *The Workhouse Ward* by Lady Gregory and Douglas Hyde. Same theatre and location as above: 1, 2, 3, 4, 5, February 1916.

1129. *Uncle Pat* by (?) The Irish Workers' Dramatic Company, Liberty Hall, Dublin: 6 February 1916.

1130. *The Coiner* by Bernard Duffy. The National Theatre Society Ltd., Abbey Theatre, Dublin: 8, 9, 10, 11, 12 February 1916.

1131. *The Shewing Up of Blanco Posnet* by George Bernard Shaw. Same theatre and location as above: 8, 9, 10, 11, 12 February 1916.

1132. *The Orangeman* by St. John Ervine. Same theatre and location as above: 8, 9, 10, 11, 12 February 1916.

1133. *The Troth* by Rutherford Mayne. The Irish Workers' Dramatic Company, Liberty Hall, Dublin: 13 February 1916.

1134. *Spreading the News* by Lady Gregory. Same theatre and location as above: 13 February 1916.

1135. *Birthright* by T. C. Murray. The National Theatre Society Ltd., Abbey Theatre, Dublin: 15, 16, 17, 18, 19 February 1916.

1136. *The Building Fund* by William Boyle. Same theatre and location as above: 15, 16, 17, 18, 19 February 1916.

1137. *The Prodigal Daughter* by Francis Sheehy-Skeffington. Performed by actors from the Abbey Theatre and the Irish Theatre Company, benefit for the Irish Citizen, Foresters' Hall, 41 Parnell Square, Dublin: 20 February 1916.

1138. *Uncle Pat* by (?) The Irish Workers' Dramatic Company, Liberty Hall, Dublin: 20 February 1916.

1139. *The Dreamers* by Lennox Robinson. The National Theatre Society Ltd., Abbey Theatre, Dublin: 22, 23, 24, 25, 26 February 1916.

1140. *Owen* by Padraic Pearse, translated by (?) Michael and John's Players, the Hall, 41 York Street, Dublin: 25, 26 February 1916.

1141. *Birthright* by T. C. Murray. The Irish Workers' Dramatic Company, Liberty Hall, Dublin: 27 February 1916.

1142. *The Lad from Largymore* by Seumas MacManus. Same theatre and location as above: 27 February 1916.

1143. *Easter* by August Strindberg. The Irish Theatre Company, Hardwicke Street Hall, Dublin: 3, 4, 5, 6, 7 March 1916.

1144. *Mixed Marriage* by St. John Ervine. The National Theatre Society Ltd., Abbey Theatre, Dublin: 7, 9, 10, 11 March 1916.

1145. *Kathleen Ni Houlihan* by W. B. Yeats. Same theatre and location as above: 7, 8, 9, 10, 11 March 1916.

1146. *The Country Dressmaker* by George Fitzmaurice. Same theatre and location as above: 14, 15, 16, 17, 18 March 1916.

1147. *The Coiner* by Bernard Duffy. Same theatre and location as above: 14, 15, 16, 17, 18 March 1916.

1148. *The Building Fund* by William Boyle. The Irish Workers' Dramatic Company, Liberty Hall, Dublin: 19 March 1916.

1149. *The Man Who Missed the Tide* by W. F. Casey. The National Theatre Society Ltd., Abbey Theatre, Dublin: 21, 22, 23, 24, 25 March 1916.

1150. *A Minute's Wait* by Martin J. McHugh. Same theatre and location as above: 21, 22, 23, 24, 25 March 1916.

1151. *Under Which Flag* by James Connolly. The Irish Workers' Dramatic Company, Liberty Hall, Dublin: 26 March 1916.

1152. *Hyacinth Halvey* by Lady Gregory. The National Theatre Society Ltd., Abbey Theatre, Dublin: 28, 29, 30, 31 March and 1 April 1916.

1153. *The Plough-Lifters* by John Guinan. Same theatre and location as above: 28, 29, 30, 31 March and 1 April 1916.

1154. *The Rising of the Moon* by Lady Gregory. Same theatre and location as above: 28, 29, 30, 31 March and 1 April 1916.

1155. One play by Constance Markievicz, title currently unknown. The Irish Workers' Dramatic Company, Liberty Hall, Dublin: 2 April 1916.

1156. *Uncle Pat* by (?). Same theatre and location as above: 1 April 1916.

1157. One play by Constance Markievicz, title currently unknown. The Irish Workers' Dramatic Company, Liberty Hall, Dublin: 9 April 1916.

1158. *Roisin's Robe* by P. Hogan. Same theatre and location as above: 23 April 1916.

1159. *The Leadin' Road* by Seumas MacManus. Same theatre and location as above: 23 April 1916.

It is unlikely that the two immediately above productions were actually performed on these dates, given that Liberty Hall was the command center for the rebel leaders on the eve of the Easter Rising. Of course, the Rising was originally planned to commence on 23 April, making their stagings even more doubtful. It is possible that the productions were advertised to provide a "cover" for the Rising's preparations that were being carried out throughout the weekend in Liberty Hall.

The following were scheduled for Easter Week, but were canceled due to the Easter Rising.

1160. *Kathleen Ni Houlihan* by W. B. Yeats. The National Theatre Society Ltd., Abbey Theatre, 24 April 1916.

1161. *The Mineral Workers* by William Boyle. Scheduled for the same theatre and location as above: 24 April 1916.

1162. *Kathleen Ni Houlihan* by W. B. Yeats. Scheduled for the same theatre and location as above: 25, 26, 27, 28, 29 April 1916.

1163. *The Spancel of Death* by T. H. Nally. Scheduled for the same theatre and location as above: 25, 26, 27, 28, 29 April 1916.

Works Cited

Fay, Frank. "*Wolfe Tone* at the Queen's Theatre." *The United Irishman.* 26 August 1899, 5.

Gregory, Lady Augusta. *Lady Gregory's Diaries, 1892–1902.* James Pethica, ed. Gerrards Cross, Buckinghamshire: Colin Smythe, 1996.

Grene, Nicholas. *The Politics of Irish Drama: Plays in Context from Boucicault to Friel.* Cambridge: Cambridge University Press, 1999.

Hogan, Robert and James Kilroy. *The Laying of the Foundations, 1902–1904.* Dublin: Dolmen Press, 1976.

———, with Richard Burnham and Daniel P. Poteet. *The Abbey Theatre: The Rise of the Realists, 1910–1915.* Dublin: Dolmen Press, 1979.

Holloway, Joseph. *Joseph Holloway's Abbey Theatre; A Selection from his Unpublished Journal "Impressions of a Dublin Playgoer."* Robert Hogan and Michael J. O'Neill, ed. Carbondale: Southern Illinois University Press, 1967.

"The Land She Loved." *The Workers' Republic.* 27 November 1915, 3.

Nic Shiubhlaigh, Maire. *The Splendid Years: Recollections of Maire Nic Shiubhlaigh as told to Edward Kenny.* Dublin: James Duffy, 1955.

Rooney, William "All Ireland." *The United Irishman.* 11 March 1899, 1.

Watt, Stephen. *Joyce, O'Casey and the Irish Popular Theatre.* Syracuse: Syracuse University Press, 1991.

Whitbread, J. W. *Wolfe Tone. For the Land She Loved.* Cheryl Herr, ed. Syracuse: Syracuse University Press, 1991.

Yeats, John B. "Out of the Dock." *The United Irishman.* 10 October 1903: 2.

Index

The, following entries include authors, play titles, and producing organizations. The numbers following each entry indicate the sequential number of the given production, not a page number.

Abbey Theatre, see Irish National Theatre Society and National Theatre Society Limited.
AE, 14, 18, 28, 60, 62, 93, 284, 617.
Aine agus Caoimhin, 531.
Airgael Croise Caoile, 51.
All-Ireland Temperance Bazaar, 97.
An tAthrughadh Mor, 191, 197, 212, 243, 263.
An Cleamhnas, 69, 1118.
An Comhrae, 386.
An Doctuir, 66, 82, 98, 102, 853, 956.
An Enchanted Sea, 96, 319, 851, 1108, 1114.
An Mi-Adh Mor, 54.
An Naomh ar Iarraid, 38, 42, 57, 507.
An tOide as Tir na nOg, 532, 574.
An Posadh, 25, 39, 91, 95, 148, 679, 877
An Ri, 744, 861, 864.
An Scrabhadoir, 425.
An Seabhac, 714.

An tSnaidhm, 1077, 1084.
An tSnaihm, 534.
An Spirit, see *An Sprid*.
An Sprid, 27, 41.
An Tailliar Cleasach, 43.
An Talinf, 192.
An Tincear Agus An tSidheog, 21, 142, 168, 504, 655, 712, 829.
An Tobar Draoidheachta, 35, 48.
The Annunciation, 700.
Aodh ONeill, 40, 52, 67.
Ar Son Baile Agus Tire, 20, 23.
Ar Thaoibh an Locha, 320.
The Aughrim National School, 710.
Author! Author!, 1109, 1115.
The Bailiff of Kilmore, 207, 560.

Bairbre Ruadh, 319, 851, 1108, 1114.
Ballian Dramatic Club, 99.
Barden, Hugh, 391, 399.
The Bargain, 1058.
Barlow, James, 694.

Beaslai, Piaras, 944, 1083, 1100.
Before Clonmel, 274.
The Bending of the Bough, 5.
Birmingham, George A., 692.
Birthright, 568, 612, 660, 723, 789, 819, 833, 846, 905, 1006, 1135, 1141.
The Bishop's Candlestick, 1118.
Blind, 778.
Bong Tong Come to Balriddery, 368.
Boycotting, 149, 158.
Boyle, William, 136, 167, 174, 185, 195, 198, 202, 214, 216, 218, 453, 467, 470, 498, 506, 519, 541, 543, 573 584, 586, 587, 620, 625, 627, 645, 658, 668, 677, 705, 728, 729, 739, 756, 766, 798, 801, 838, 842, 870, 880, 885, 894, 921, 924, 928, 931, 997, 1003, 1007, 1018, 1046, 1052, 1057, 1067, 1069, 1090, 1091, 1123, 1136, 1148, 1161.
Branch of the Five Provinces, 189.
Brian of Banba, 114.
The Bribe, 925, 939, 987, 1011, 1127.
The Brinsley Sheridan Players, 1093.
Broken Faith, 849, 894.
Broken Soil, 84.
The Building Fund, 136, 185, 202, 453, 470, 498, 541, 584, 627, 705, 801, 838, 885, 924, 1007, 1067, 1102, 1136, 1148.
Bullock, Shan, F., 1040.
A Bunch of Lavenda, 694.
Butler, Mary E. L., 22.
The Burden, 518.
By Word of Mouth, 1037.

Caitlin Ni hCallachain, 143, 719, 742, 911.
The Call to Arms, 561.
Campbell, Joseph, 137, 735.

The Canavans, 201, 206, 276, 281, 474, 713, 892, 945.
Candidates, 967.
Captains of the Hosts, 492.
Casadh an tSugain, 13, 63, 110, 203, 862, 1076.
Casey, W. F., 287, 306, 326, 333, 341, 347, 370, 374, 382, 387, 396, 434, 442, 494, 545, 559, 590, 604, 634, 741, 763, 902, 916, 992, 1000, 1021, 1049, 1054, 1117, 1149.
The Casting Out of Martin Whelan, 557, 817, 840, 876, 1035.
The Catholic Boys' Brigade, 100.
Cave Hill Social Club of Belfast, 26.
Celtic Literary Society, 16.
The Challenge, 441.
Chapelizod Dramatic Class, 368.
Charity, 683.
Chekhov, Anton, see Anton Tchekoff.
Child, Dixon, 779.
Christie, R. A., 991, 998.
The Clancy Name, 335, 352, 437, 585, 676, 937, 1072.
The Claham School, 714.
Cluiche Cartai, 986.
Cluithcheoiri na hEireann, 192, 203, 204, 227, 228, 244, 245, 284, 285, 311, 312, 313, 318, 360, 361, 366, 367, 389, 390, 407, 408, 456, 457, 458, 484, 485, 489, 502, 503, 531, 610, 623, 624, 680, 694, 695, 736, 737, 742, 743, 745, 982, 983.
Coats, 383, 607, 752, 781, 929.
The Cobweb, 1002, 1020.
The Coiner, 1130, 1147.
Colum, Padraic, 56, 84, 141, 156, 162, 192, 227, 244, 271, 279, 311, 477, 508, 515, 563, 621, 769.

The Coming of Aideen, 522, 670.
The Coming of Fionn, 510.
Connell, Norreys, 288, 334, 348, 395, 410, 412, 418, 435, 556, 609, 663, 764, 887, 915.
Connolly, James, 1151.
Connolly, Joseph, 882, 914.
Cooney, R., 778.
The Cork Dramatic Society, 411, 464, 465, 466, 517, 518, 570, 571, 592, 593, 594, 636, 637, 638, 639, 649, 650, 651, 688, 689, 730, 731, 732, 733, 783, 784, 785, 786, 787, 811, 812.
The Cork National Theatre, 111, 112, 127, 128, 129, 165.
Corkery, Daniel, 411, 465, 570, 592, 636, 651, 688, 732, 783, 785.
Costello, Fr. J. M., 800, 802, 805, 813.
Costello, Mary, 522, 523, 670, 769.
The Countess Cathleen, 1, 690, 758.
The Country Dressmaker, 269, 762, 804, 828, 844, 878, 938, 1005, 1042, 1146.
Cousins, James, 30, 34, 50, 74, 79, 80, 92, 165, 193, 204, 242, 616, 696.
Cox, Watty, 695.
Cregan, James, 562.
Creideamh agus Gorta, 147.
The Cricket on the Hearth, 614.
The Critic, 1026, 1028.
The Critics, or a New Play at the Abbey, 907, 926.
The Croke Club, 955, 956.
Crone, William, 1058.
The Cross Roads, 393, 409, 439, 475, 536, 575, 606, 647, 662.
The Crossing, 786, 996.
Cuaird na Bainroghna, 530.
The Cuckoo's Nest, 827, 831, 874.
Cumann Ceoil Drama, 52.
Cumann na nGaedhael Irish Theatre Company (see also the National Players Society), 76, 77, 78, 79, 80, 81, 90, 91, 92, 95.
Cummings, G. D., 849, 894.

Damer's Gold, 777, 867, 897.
The Dangerous Age, 716.
The Dark Hour, 991, 998.
David Mahony, 947.
A Daughter of Ireland, 591, 640.
Day, S. R., 760, 849, 883, 894.
The Davis Players, 958.
The Dawn of Common Sense, 950.
The Dean of St. Patrick, 810, 824, 835, 890.
de l'Isle Adam, Villers, 1030.
Deirdre (AE's), 14, 18, 28, 60, 62, 93, 284, 617.
Deirdre (Fr. O'Kelly's), 423, 458.
Deirdre (W. B. Yeats'), 200, 260, 349, 481, 499, 605, 635, 674.
Deirdre of the Sorrows, 471, 513.
The Deliverance of Red Hugh, 9, 104, 211.
The Deliverer, 599.
Derrorgilla, 275, 280, 316, 337, 354, 706, 806.
Destruction of Da Derga's Hostel, 477, 508.
Dever, John, 187, 226.
The Devil's Disciple, 859.
Diarmuid and Grannia, 12.
The Dilettante, 364.
Dinneen, Fr., 35, 48.
Dochtuireacht Nuadh, 58.
The Doctor in Spite of Himself, 183, 230, 246, 307, 344, 476.
Dowling, Miss, 979.
Down in Kerry, 618.
Doyle, Lynn, 909, 962, 980.
Drama Breith Criosta, 120, 595.
Dramatic Class of Cumann Li-tiordha Colmchille, 43.

The Dramatic Society of the I. C. I.
C. Y. M. A., 778, 779, 780.
The Draper's Dramatic Society, 187, 226.
The Dream Maker, 780.
The Dream Physician, 1008, 1044.
The Dreamers, 1043, 1139.
Drift, 787.
The Drone 303, 346, 462, 491, 684, 964, 1023, 1097.
Dubhairt se Dabhairt se, 714.
The Dublin Amateur Operatic Society, 504, 521.
Duffy, Bernard, 1116, 1120, 1130, 1147.
Duncan, James, 17, 381.
Dunsany, Lord, 406, 415, 449, 505, 520, 565, 603, 628, 644, 770.
Duty, 922, 927, 990, 1012, 1055, 1096.

Easter, 1143.
Eithne, 424, 521.
Eleanor's Enterprise, 692.
Elis agus Bhean Deirce, 10, 32.
The Eloquent Dempsey, 167, 174, 198, 218, 467, 506, 519, 586, 620, 645, 658, 739, 756, 889, 928, 997, 1046, 1069, 1090, 1091.
The Embers, 411, 570.
Emmet and Napolean, 45.
The Enthusiast, 138, 313, 685, 963.
Ervine, St. John, 629, 633, 746, 765, 782, 856, 873, 907, 908, 926, 930, 959, 971, 1038, 1041, 1068, 1095, 1132, 1144.
The Epilogue, 651.
Evening, 957.
Exile of Erin, 1093.
The Eyes of the Blind, 252, 264.

Family Failing, 729, 766, 880, 931, 934, 1018, 1052.
Family Rights, 794.

Fand, 265.
Farquhar, George, 1086.
Fate of the Children, 318.
A Feis at Ancient Tara, 656.
Fell, Marian, 1031.
Ferguson, Sir Samuel, 493.
Fianna Players of the Fianna Eireann, 865.
The Fiddler's House, 227, 244.
Finnigan, Thomas, 1093.
Fitzmaurice, George, 269, 296, 383, 579, 619, 672, 757, 762, 804, 828, 844, 850, 878, 895, 938, 1005, 1042, 1146.
Fitzpatrick, Kathleen, 485.
Fitzpatrick, Nora, 365, 527, 716.
The Flame on the Earth (It is possible that this is Seumas O'Kelly's play *The Flame on the Hearth*) 489.
The Flame on the Hearth, 361, 366, 390.
Flanagan, W. P., 1037.
The Flight into Egypt, 701.
Ford, Joseph, 560.
Frank Fay Poetry Reading, 16.
Fraternity, 1116, 1120.

Gaelic Athletic Association, 42.
Gaelic Class Students, 979.
Gaelic League Branch Theatres, 6, 13, 15, 20, 25, 27, 35, 39, 40, 41, 48, 53, 63, 68, 69, 75, 86, 101, 120, 142, 143, 144, 146, 147, 155, 168, 169, 190, 225, 263, 319, 320, 321, 322, 359, 386, 421, 423, 424, 425, 530, 532, 533, 534, 546, 547, 548, 549, 550, 551, 552, 553, 554, 574, 653, 654, 655, 656, 719, 720, 851, 852, 853, 862, 863, 932, 943, 944, 950, 951, 985, 986, 1079, 1083, 1084, 1100, 1101.

A Gallant of Galway, 17.
A Gallant of Galway (revised), 381.
Galloping O'Hogan, 175.
The Gaol Gate, 194, 236, 258, 289, 327, 372, 379, 469, 544, 816, 879, 923.
Gilbert, Lady, 149, 158.
Glesson, 59, 86.
The Glittering Gate, 406, 415, 449, 505, 520, 565, 628, 644, 770.
The Gods at Play, 523, 796.
The Golden Helmet, 297, 330, 479, 525, 1056.
Goldini, Carlo, 486, 578, 969, 972.
The Gombeen Man, 900, 935.
The Gomeril, 408.
The Good People, 698.
Gore-Booth, Eva, 709.
Grangecolman, 708.
Graves, Arnold, 369.
Gregory, Lady, 47, 88, 134, 135, 157, 171, 183, 186, 194, 196, 201, 206, 219, 221, 230, 232, 233, 234, 236, 237, 246, 248, 249, 253, 254, 255, 256, 257, 258, 272, 275, 276, 277, 280, 281, 282, 283, 289, 292, 295, 298, 299, 301, 302, 305, 307, 309, 315, 316, 317, 323, 325, 327, 328, 329, 332, 337, 340, 342, 344, 350, 354, 357, 358, 362, 363, 371, 372, 373, 376, 377, 378, 379, 385, 394, 402, 404, 405, 417, 427, 429, 433, 438, 440, 443, 445, 446, 448, 454, 455, 461, 469, 472, 474, 476, 482, 486, 487, 488, 495, 496, 500, 514, 535, 537, 544, 558, 564, 566, 567, 569, 576, 578, 581, 583, 588, 595, 596, 599, 600, 602, 607, 608, 622, 626, 648, 661, 664, 666, 667, 679, 702, 703, 706, 707, 711, 713, 718, 724, 734, 747, 749, 752, 754, 759, 768, 772, 775, 777, 781, 790, 791, 806, 807, 809, 816, 820, 822, 830, 834, 843, 847, 858, 867, 868, 872, 877, 879, 886, 892, 897, 901, 903, 906, 917, 920, 923, 929, 936, 945, 948, 961, 969, 970, 972, 973, 976, 977, 1010, 1019, 1034, 1048, 1050, 1060, 1124, 1128, 1134, 1152, 1154.
Guinan, John, 827, 831, 874, 1153.

Hamilton, John, 109.
Hannele, 823, 837, 884.
The Hard-Hearted Man, 100, 107, 123, 163, 169, 178.
Harding, Robert. 304, 345.
The Harp That Once, 8.
Harvest, 524, 601, 665.
Hauptmann, Gerhardt, 823, 837, 884.
The Heather Field, 2, 64, 398.
Her Second Chance, 984.
The Hermit and the King, 465, 592, 732.
Hobson, Bulmer, 114.
Hogan, P., 1125, 1158.
The Holocaust, 594, 649.
The Home Coming (Seumas O'Kelly), 503.
The Home Coming (Gertrude Robins), 839.
Home Sweet Home, 365, 527.
Honor's Choice, 652.
The Hospital Ward, 671.
The Hour Glass, 46, 83, 140, 170, 213, 215, 278, 291, 356, 598, 776.
How He Lied to Her Husband, 983.
Hugh ONeill, 67,103.
Hugh Roe O'Donnell, 26.
Hurson, George J., 591, 640.

Hyacinth Halvey, 171, 219, 237, 257, 277, 298, 357, 394, 402, 417, 496, 535, 581, 666, 734, 772, 807, 906, 970, 973, 1019, 1152.

Hyde, Douglas, 13, 21, 25, 38, 39, 42, 55, 57, 63, 69, 78, 91, 95, 110, 120, 121, 130, 142, 148, 151, 168, 203, 302, 305, 315, 362, 404, 429, 438, 445, 461, 482, 500, 504, 507, 558, 595, 622, 655, 664, 679, 703, 712, 724, 820, 829, 834, 847, 862, 877, 917, 936, 952, 1034, 1076, 1128.

If, 910, 1022.

The Image, 454, 488, 608.

An Imaginary Conversation, 413, 418.

The Independent Dramatic Company, 293, 364, 365, 511, 512, 526, 527, 631.

The Independent Theatre Company, 692, 693, 708, 709, 715, 716, 760.

Inghinidhe na hEireann, 8, 9, 10, 11, 18, 19, 38, 42, 54, 55, 56, 57, 58, 59, 450.

Interior, 239, 247, 473, 572.

The Interlude of Youth, 678.

The International Exhibition, 108.

Iosagan, 478, 509, 1074.

The Irish Historical Players, 800, 802, 805, 813.

The Irish Literary Theatre, 1, 2, 3, 4, 5, 12, 13.

Irish National Theatre Society Limited, 24, 28, 29, 30, 31, 32, 33, 34, 36, 37, 45, 46, 47, 49, 50, 60, 61, 62, 70, 72, 83, 87, 88, 89, 93, 94, 116, 117, 118, 119, 125, 134, 135, 136, 140, 141.

The Irish Players, 952, 953, 954.

The Irish Socialist Republican Party, 49.

Irish Tableaux Vivants, 7, 11, 450, 1085.

Irish Theatrical Club, 369, 522, 523.

The Irish Theatre Company, 1008, 1029, 1030, 1031, 1032, 1044, 1062, 1063, 1076, 1077, 1078, 1080, 1082, 1087, 1106, 1107, 1108, 1109, 1112, 1113, 1114, 1115, 1119, 1137, 1143.

The Irish Theatre and National Stage Society, 652, 669, 670, 671.

The Irish Workers' Dramatic Company, 799, 1081, 1090, 1099, 1102, 1105, 1118, 1122, 1129, 1133, 1134, 1138, 1141, 1142, 1148, 1151, 1155, 1156, 1157, 1158, 1159.

The Irish Workers' Union, 1086.

The Irishwomen's Reform League, 883.

Israel's Incense, 783.

The Jackdaw, 233, 255, 317, 328, 342, 448, 495, 514, 602, 661, 790, 948, 1048.

Jay, F., 1002, 1020.

The Jerrybuilder's, 687.

John Ferguson, 1094.

Judgement, 735.

The Jug of Sorrow, 1004, 1015.

Kathleen Ni Houlihan, 19, 29, 72, 73, 76, 118, 128, 143, 172, 199, 222, 231, 240, 261, 267, 324, 331, 375, 380, 388, 397, 401, 430, 452, 459, 539, 597, 632, 657, 719, 742, 750, 788, 818, 832, 845, 891, 911, 933, 949, 958, 1025, 1027, 1145, 1160, 1162.

Kearney, Peter, 561.

Keating Gaelic League Branch, see Gaelic League Branch Theatres.

Kelleher, D. L., 384.

Kelly, Fr., see Fr. O'Kelly.
Kennedy, Mrs. Bart, 888.
Kincora, 134, 135, 376, 405, 976.
King Argimenes and the Unknown Warrior, 603.
The King's Threshold, 70, 896, 941.
Kinship, 968.
Kitty, 22.
Knocknagow, 836, 1064.

Labhraidh, A., 1077, 1084.
The Lad from Largymore, 126, 131, 150, 160, 164, 177, 1080, 1119, 1142.
Ladies Committee of Feis Ceoil, 966, 967.
The Land, 141, 192, 271, 279.
The Land of Heart's Desire, 611, 717, 854.
The Last of the Desmonds, 127.
The Last Feast of the Fianna, 4, 189, 228, 245.
The Last Irish King, 111.
The Last Warriors, 571.
The Last Warriors of Coole, 638.
The Laying of the Foundations, 31, 37, 49.
Leaders of the People, 304, 345.
The Leadin' Road to Donegal, 154, 155, 1122, 1159.
The Leinster Stage Society, 528, 614, 615, 616, 617, 696, 697, 698, 699.
The Lesson of His Life, 466, 593, 650.
Letts, Winifred M., 252, 264, 441.
A Little Christmas Miracle, 797.
The Little Cowherd of Slainge, 137.
Lloyd, Annie, J. W., 966.
The Lord Mayor, 960, 975, 1073, 1103, 1110.
Love and Land, 909, 962, 980.
The Love Charm, 668.
Lover, Samuel, 179, 210.

Lucy, D. P., 730, 784.
Lyons, John F., 787.

M., Joseph, see J. Malachi Muldoon.
Mac Carthaigh Mor, 321.
MacCarthy, Brian, 618.
MacCarthy, J. Bernard, 780, 811, 812, 968, 989.
MacDaragh's Wife (later *McDonogh's Wife*), 702, 920.
MacDomhnaill, Tomas, 531.
MacDonagh, Thomas, 339, 736, 1063.
MacDonagh, John, 1109, 1115.
MacFhionnlaioch, P. T., (see P. T. MacGinley).
MacGinley, P. T., 10, 32, 43, 58.
McHugh, Martin J., 988, 1001, 1014, 1053, 1059, 1104, 1111, 1150.
Macklin, Charles, 484, 623, 982.
MacManus, L., 273, 725.
MacManus, Seumas, 89, 100, 105, 107, 113, 122, 123, 124, 126, 131, 132, 150, 153, 154, 155, 160, 161, 163, 164, 169, 177, 178, 188, 368, 1080, 1119, 1122, 1142, 1159.
McNulty, Edward, 960, 975, 1073, 1103, 1110.
Mac na Mna Deirce, 852.
MacNamara, Gerald, 463, 490, 793, 815, 981, 1024, 1098.
MacRury, Michael, 852.
MacSwiney, Terrence, 571, 637, 638, 649, 689.
Maeterlinck, Maurice, 239, 247, 473, 572.
Maeve, 3, 312.
The Magic Glasses, 850, 895.
The Magic Sieve, 109.
The Magnanimous Lover, 765, 856, 873, 1041, 1068.
Maistin an Bhearla, 952.

The Man Who Missed the Tide, 287, 306, 326, 341, 374, 387, 434, 494, 559, 604, 634, 741, 916, 1000, 1049.
Mangan, Henry Connell, 45, 77, 90, 133, 262.
Manners Maketh Man, 637.
A Man's Foes, 80, 92.
Maol, Conan, 40, 52.
Markham, Thomas, 139.
Markievicz, Count Casimir, 293, 364, 365, 511, 512, 526, 527, 631, 693, 715.
Markievicz, Countess, Constance, 1155, 1157.
The Marriage of Julia Elizabeth, 681.
Martyn, Edward, 2, 3, 64, 96, 152, 312, 398, 708, 1008, 1044, 1087.
Mary, 512.
The Master, 1075.
The Matchmaker, 285, 457, 955, 1099, 1126.
Maurice Harte, 753, 774, 857, 994, 1016, 1065, 1088.
A May Eve in Stephen's Green, 1101.
Maynooth College Students, 51.
The Memory of the Dead, 511, 526, 631, 715.
The Men in Possession, 811.
The Message, 528.
Metempsychosis, 736.
Metropolitan School of Art Students, 391, 392, 399, 400, 529.
Michael and John's Players, 1140.
Milligan, Alice, 4, 8, 9, 104, 127, 189, 211, 228, 245, 431.
The Mine Land, 882, 914.
The Mineral Workers, 195, 214, 216, 543, 573, 587, 625, 677, 728, 798, 842, 870, 921, 1003, 1057, 1123, 1161.
A Minute's Wait, 988, 1001, 1014, 1053, 1104, 1111, 1150.

Mirandolina, 486, 578, 969, 972.
The Miracle of the Corn, 311.
The Miser, 373, 378, 446, 566.
The Mist That Does Be on the Bog, 463, 490, 981.
Mixed Marriage, 629, 633, 746, 782, 908, 930, 1038, 1144.
Moliere, 183, 230, 246, 299, 307, 325, 340, 344, 350, 373, 378, 385, 446, 476, 566, 596.
Moore, E. Hamilton, 797.
Moore, George, 5, 12, 59, 86.
Moore, T. C., 1037.
Moylan, Thomas King, 392, 400, 529.
Muirgheis, 59, 86.
Muldoon, J. Malachi, 641, 671.
Mulholland, Rosa, 149, 158.
Murray, T. C, 464, 568, 612, 660, 723, 753, 774, 789, 819, 833, 846, 857, 875, 904, 905, 940, 994, 995, 1006, 1016, 1036, 1061, 1065, 1088, 1089, 1135, 1141.
My Lord, 888.
The Naboclish, 529.

Nally, T. H., 1163.
The Naming of Cuchullain, 493.
The Nation Builders, 129.
National Council, 431.
National Literary Society, 17, 50.
National Players Society, 95, 104, 105, 106, 107, 108, 109, 113, 121, 122, 123, 124, 126, 130, 131, 132, 145, 148, 149, 150, 151, 152, 153, 154, 156, 158, 159, 160, 161, 162, 163, 164.
National Players, 177, 178, 179, 188, 193, 197, 210, 211, 212, 241, 242, 243.
National Theatre Society Limited, 157, 166, 170, 171, 172, 173, 174, 176, 182, 183, 184, 185,

Index 123

National Theatre Society Limited, *(continued)*
186, 194, 195, 196, 198, 199, 200, 201, 202, 205, 206, 213, 214, 215, 216, 217, 218, 219, 220, 221, 222, 223, 224, 229, 230, 231, 232, 233, 234, 235, 236, 237, 238, 239, 240, 246, 247, 248, 249, 252, 253, 254, 255, 256, 257, 258, 259, 260, 261, 264, 265, 266, 267, 268, 269, 270, 271, 272, 275, 276, 277, 278, 279, 280, 281, 282, 283, 287, 288, 289, 290, 291, 294, 295, 296, 297, 298, 299, 300, 301, 302, 305, 306, 307, 308, 309, 310, 314, 315, 316, 317, 323, 324, 325, 326, 327, 328, 329, 330, 331, 332, 333, 334, 335, 336, 337, 338, 339, 340, 341, 342, 344, 347, 348, 349, 350, 351, 352, 353, 354, 355, 356, 357, 358, 362, 370, 371, 372, 373, 374, 376, 377, 378, 379, 380, 382, 383, 384, 385, 387, 388, 393, 394, 395, 396, 397, 398, 401, 402, 403, 404, 405, 406, 409, 410, 412, 413, 414, 415, 416, 417, 418, 419, 426, 427, 428, 429, 430, 432, 433, 434, 435, 436, 437, 438, 439, 440, 441, 442, 443, 444, 445, 446, 447, 448, 449, 451, 452, 453, 454, 455, 459, 460, 461, 468, 469, 470, 471, 472, 473, 474, 475, 476, 479, 480, 481, 482, 483, 486, 487, 488, 494, 495, 496, 497, 498, 499, 500, 501, 505, 506, 513, 514, 515, 516, 519, 520, 524, 525, 535, 536, 537, 538, 539, 540, 541, 542, 543, 544, 545, 555, 556, 557, 558, 559, 563, 564, 565, 566, 567, 568, 569, 572, 573, 575, 576, 577, 578, 579, 580, 581, 582, 583, 584, 585, 586, 587, 588, 589, 590, 595, 596, 597, 598, 599, 600, 601, 602, 603, 604, 605, 606, 607, 608, 609, 611, 612, 613, 619, 620, 621, 622, 625, 626, 627, 628, 629, 632, 633, 634, 635, 642, 643, 649, 645, 646, 647, 648, 657, 658, 659, 660, 661, 662, 663, 664, 665, 666, 667, 668, 672, 673, 674, 675, 676, 677, 678, 679, 690, 691, 700, 701, 702, 703, 704, 705, 706, 707, 711, 712, 713, 717, 718, 721, 722, 723, 724, 727, 728, 729, 734, 735, 738, 739, 740, 741, 746, 747, 748, 749, 750, 751, 752, 753, 754, 755, 756, 757, 758, 759, 761, 762, 763, 764, 765, 766, 767, 768, 769, 770, 771, 772, 773, 774, 775, 776, 777, 781, 782, 788, 789, 790, 791, 792, 797, 798, 801, 803, 804, 806, 807, 808, 809, 810, 816, 817, 818, 819, 820, 821, 822, 823, 824, 825, 826, 827, 828, 829, 830, 831, 832, 833, 834, 835, 837, 838, 839, 840, 841, 842, 843, 844, 845, 846, 847, 848, 849, 850, 854, 855, 856, 857, 858, 860, 866, 867, 868, 869, 870, 871, 872, 873, 874, 875, 876, 877, 878, 879, 880, 881, 882, 884, 885, 886, 887, 888, 889, 890, 891, 892, 893, 894, 895, 896, 897, 898, 899, 900, 901, 902, 904, 905, 906, 907, 908, 914, 915, 916, 917, 918, 919, 920, 921, 922, 923, 924, 925, 926, 927, 928, 929, 930, 931, 933,

National Theatre Society Limited, *(continued)*
    934, 935, 936, 937, 938, 940, 941, 942, 945, 946, 947, 948, 949, 959, 960, 968, 969, 970, 971, 972, 973, 974, 975, 976, 977, 987, 988, 989, 990, 991, 992, 993, 994, 995, 996, 997, 998, 999, 1000, 1001, 1002, 1003, 1004, 1005, 1006, 1007, 1009, 1010, 1011, 1012, 1013, 1014, 1015, 1016, 1017, 1018, 1019, 1020, 1021, 1025, 1027, 1028, 1033, 1034, 1035, 1036, 1037, 1038, 1041, 1042, 1043, 1045, 1046, 1047, 1048, 1049, 1050, 1052, 1053, 1054, 1055, 1056, 1057, 1058, 1059, 1060, 1061, 1065, 1066, 1067, 1068, 1069, 1070, 1071, 1072, 1073, 1088, 1089, 1091, 1092, 1094, 1095, 1096, 1103, 1104, 1110, 1111, 1116, 1117, 1120, 1121, 1123, 1124, 1125, 1126, 1127, 1128, 1130, 1131, 1132, 1135, 1136, 1137, 1139, 1144, 1145, 1146, 1147, 1149, 1150, 1152, 1153, 1154, 1160, 1161, 1162, 1163.
The New Ireland Dramatic Society, 560, 561, 562.
Ni Cinneide, Marie, 322, 653.

O Ceallaig, An Tatair, 320.
O Ladpraid, Alponr, 534.
O nAoda, Tomas, 101, 106, 146, 190, 654.
O'Beirne, Seumas, 66, 82, 98, 102, 853, 956.
O'Brennan, Lily M., 1101.
O'Brien, Cruise, 967.
O'Brien, Seumas, 922, 927, 990, 1012, 1055, 1096.
O'Brien Butler, 59, 86.
O'Conaire, Padraig, 319, 851, 1108, 1114.
O'Domhnaill, Liam, 1029.
O'Donnell's Cross, 273, 725.
O'Dorney, 20, 23.
O'Duffy, Eimar, 1032, 1062, 1107, 1113.
O'Dwyer, Robert, 424, 521.
O'E., J., 502.
O'Friel, Morgan, 615, 697.
O'Grady, Standish, 26, 510.
O'Hanlon, H. B., 984.
O'Heran, Seumas, 699.
Oighreacht Roisin, 533.
O'Kelly, Fr., 143, 423, 424, 458, 521, 719, 911.
O'Kelly, Seumas, 285, 361, 366, 390, 407, 456, 457, 503, 580, 852, 925, 939, 955, 987, 1011,1099,1126,1127.
O'Leary, Con, 517, 731, 786, 996.
O'Leary, Fr., 6, 27, 41, 53, 75, 159.
O'Loughlin, Gerald, 241.
O'Loughlin, John, 129.
O' Murthuile, Sean, 985.
O'Neill, Eamonn, 15, 67, 103.
O'Neill Russell, T., 111, 180, 181.
On Baile's Strand, 116, 182, 238.
The Onus of Ownership, 636, 688, 785.
The Orangeman, 959, 971, 1132.
The Ordeal of David, 745.
O Seagda, Padraig, 321, 533, 743.
Ostrovsky, Aleksandr, 610.
O'Toole, E. L., 68.
Out of the Deep Shadow, 760.
Owen, 1140.

The Pagan, 209, 250.
Pagans, 1063.
Paid in His Own Coin, 392, 400.
Parkhill, Davis, see Lewis Purcell.
The Passing of 'Miah, 730, 784.

A Passion Play, 630.
Paternoster, G. Sidney, 810, 824, 835, 890.
Patriots, 733, 748, 771, 855, 889, 919, 1033, 1095.
Paul, William, 687, 795, 814.
Pearse, Margaret (M. B.), 528, 614, 698.
Pearse, Padraic, 478, 509, 630, 744, 861, 864, 1074, 1075, 1140.
The Philosopher, 1059.
The Phoenix on the Roof, 1032, 1107.
The Pie-dish, 296, 383, 579, 619, 672, 757.
Pioneer Dramatic Society, 181, 467, 591, 640, 641, 725, 726, 836.
The Piper, 288, 334, 348, 435, 556, 609, 663, 764, 887, 915.
The Playboy of the Western World, 223, 419, 426, 480, 538, 643, 751, 871, 1071.
The Players' Club, 64, 96.
Pleusgadh an Bulgoide, 55, 78, 130.
The Plough-Lifters, 1153.
The Poorhouse, 253.
Posadh an Iasgaine, 985.
The Post Office, 860, 881.
The Pot of Broth, 33, 36, 61, 85, 112, 229, 266, 355, 451, 468, 516, 613, 727, 773, 821.
Power, Victor, O'D., 745, 947.
The Privilege of Place, 1087.
Pro Patria, 669.
The Prodigal, 999, 1121.
The Prodigal Daughter, 978, 1137.
P'Seagda, Padraig, 321, 533, 743.
Purcell, Lewis, 115, 138, 209, 250, 286, 313, 685, 737, 963.

A Question of Honor, 966.

The Racing Lug, 34, 74, 204, 616, 696.

The Rapparee, 241.
Ray, R. J., 432, 557, 817, 840, 876, 900, 935, 1035.
The Recruiting Officer, 1086.
Red Hugh, 180, 181.
Red Turf, 686, 704, 803.
Redmond, Johanna, 652, 669, 710, 726.
The Reformers, 115, 737.
The Repertory Theatre, 859.
The Resurrection of Dinny O'Dowd, 105, 113, 122, 124, 132, 161, 188.
The Return of Columbkille, 800, 802, 805, 813.
The Return of Lugh Lamb Fada, 431.
The Revolt, 1030.
Riddall, Walter, 999, 1121.
Riders to the Sea, 94, 166, 173, 217, 224, 259, 308, 416, 444, 452, 577, 642, 738, 755, 808, 826, 898, 1070.
The Rising of the Moon, 234, 248, 254, 272, 292, 301, 323, 329, 358, 376, 377, 427, 440, 455, 472, 537, 564, 569, 588, 626, 648, 667, 707, 718, 747, 754, 775, 809, 830, 843, 858, 872, 903, 961, 1010, 1154.
Rival Stars, 693.
Robert Emmet, 77, 90, 133, 262.
Robin, Gertrude, 839.
Robinson, Lennox, 335, 352, 393, 409, 437, 439, 466, 475, 524, 536, 575, 585, 593, 601, 647, 650, 662, 665, 676, 733, 748, 771, 855, 889, 919, 937, 1033, 1043, 1072, 1095, 1139.
The Roguries of Scapin, 299, 325, 340, 350, 385, 596.
Roisin's Robe, 1125, 1158.
Rosaleen Dhu, 187, 226.
Russell, George, see AE.

Rutherford, Mayne, 208, 252, 303, 346, 360, 367, 389, 408, 462, 491, 492, 680, 684, 686, 704, 803, 910, 957, 964, 1022, 1023, 1029, 1097, 1133.
Ryan, Frederick, 31, 37, 49.
Ryan, Joseph, 81, 108.
Ryan, W. P., 54, 530, 532, 574, 1004, 1015.

The Saxon Schillin', 56, 156, 162.
The Scheming Lieutenant, 314, 338, 353.
Scott, Molly. F., 683, 794.
Seabac na Ceathramha Caoilte, 190.
Seaghan na Scuab, 101, 106, 146, 654.
Seymour's Redemption, 293.
In the Shadow of the Glen, 71, 119, 184, 220, 270, 290, 300, 336, 351, 403, 414, 497, 589, 624, 659, 722, 740, 767, 848, 869, 918, 1045, 1092.
The Shadowy Waters, 87, 205.
Shanwalla, 1060.
Shaw, George Bernard, 428, 436, 447, 460, 483, 501, 540, 582, 646, 675, 792, 859, 946, 983, 1017, 1066, 1131.
Sheehy-Skeffington, Francis, 978, 1137.
The Second Shepherd's Play, 682, 691, 761, 893.
Sheridan, Richard Brinsley, 314, 338, 353, 1026, 1028.
The Shewing up of Blanco Posnet, 428, 436, 447, 460, 483, 501, 540, 582, 646, 675, 792, 946, 1017, 1066, 1131.
The Shuiler's Child, 407, 456, 580, 852.
Sinn Fein Dramatic Society, 207, 262.

The Skull, 615, 697.
The Sleep of the King, 30.
The Slough, 1009, 1013, 1047.
Snowdrop Jane, 1040.
Sold, 165, 242.
Solus na Saoirseacht, 422.
Sovereign Love, 875, 904, 940, 995, 1036, 1061, 1089.
The Spancel of Death, 1163.
The Spoiled Buddha, 1039.
Spreading the News, 117, 186, 196, 221, 249, 256, 283, 309, 332, 433, 443, 567, 711, 714, 759, 822, 868, 901, 977, 1050, 1124, 1134.
The Spurious Queen, 502.
St. Enda's School Theatre, 477, 478, 507, 508, 509, 510, 630, 744, 861, 864, 913, 1074, 1075.
St. Mary's College Literary and Dramatic Society of Rathmines, 984.
Stella and Vanessa, 369.
Stephen Grey: A Dream and an Incident, 384.
Stephens, James, 681.
The Storm (Hugh Barden's), 391, 399.
The Storm (Aleksandr Ostrovsky's), 610.
The Stranger, 841.
Strindberg, August, 825, 841, 1143.
Struck, 517, 731.
Students of Mount Melleray, 67.
Students of St. Patrick's College, Carlow, 180.
The Suburban Groove, 333, 347, 370, 382, 396, 442, 545, 590, 763, 902, 992, 1021, 1054, 1117.
Sudermann, H., 295.
The Supplanter, 989.
Suzanne and the Sovereigns, 286.
The Swan Song, 1031, 1106, 1112.

Sweeping the Country, 795, 814.
The Sword of Dreamt, 50, 79, 193.
Synge, John M., 71, 94, 119, 125, 166, 173, 184, 217, 220, 223, 224, 259, 270, 290, 300, 308, 310, 336, 343, 351, 403, 412, 414, 416, 419, 426, 444, 471, 480, 497, 513, 538, 542, 555, 577, 589, 624, 642, 643, 659, 673, 722, 738, 740, 751, 755, 767, 808, 826, 848, 866, 871, 898, 918, 942, 1045, 1070, 1071, 1092.

Tadg Saor, 6, 53, 75, 159.
Tagore, Rabindranath, 860, 881.
The Tale of the Town, 152.
Tawin Players, 66, 82, 98, 102.
Tchekoff, Anton, 1031, 1078, 1106, 1112.
Teach na nBocht, 121, 151.
Tega, 295.
Teig Cocoran's Courtship, 562.
Tenement Troubles, 97.
Theatre of Ireland, see Cluithcheoiri na hEireann.
There are Crimes and Crimes, 825.
Thomas Muskerry, 515, 563, 621, 769.
Thompson in Tir na n'Og, 793, 815, 1024, 1098.
Time, 395, 410.
Toilers, 883.
Tohma, 192.
The Townland of Tamney, 89.
The Trail of the Serpent, 139.
The Traveling Man, 576, 600.
The Troth, 1029, 1133.
The True-Born Irishman, 484, 623, 982.
The Turn of the Road, 208, 251, 360, 367, 389, 680, 965.
Twenty-five, 47, 88.

A Twinkle in Ireland's Eye, 81.

Ua Muineachain, P., 175.
Ui Breasail Amateur Dramatic Society, 618.
The Ulster Literary Theatre, 73, 74, 114, 115, 137, 138, 208, 209, 250, 252, 286, 303, 304, 345, 346, 462, 463, 490, 491, 492, 493, 683, 684, 685, 686, 687, 793, 794, 795.
The Ulster Players, 814, 815.
The Ulster Theatre, 909, 910, 911, 912, 957, 962, 963, 964, 965, 980, 981, 1022, 1023, 1024, 1025, 1039, 1040, 1097, 1098.
Uncle Pat, 1129, 1138, 1156.
Uncle Vanya, 1078.
Under Delusion, 779.
Under Which Flag, 1151.
The Unicorn from the Stars, 282, 791.
Unseen Kings, 709.
Ursuline Convent Students, 103.

Varian, Susan, 97.
Victims, 799.

Waddell, Helen, 1039.
Waldron, Michael, 44.
The Walls of Athens, 1062.
Walsh, R. G., 274, 836, 1064.
The Well of Saints, 125, 310, 343, 412, 555, 673, 942.
A West Briton's Romance, 225.
The Western Players, 191.
The West's Awake, 641.
W. G. Fay's Amateur Acting company, 14, 18, 19.
The Wheel o' Fortune, 464.
When the Dawn Is Come, 339.
The White Cockade, 157, 232, 363, 768, 886.
The White Feather, 432.

The White Horse of the Peppers, 179, 210.
The Widow Dempsey's Funeral, 695.
Wilson, A. Patrick, 799, 974, 993, 1009, 1013, 1047.
The Woman of the Seven Sorrows, 153.
The Women's Franchise League, 978.
The Wooing of Emer, 689.
The Workhouse Ward, 302, 305, 315, 362, 404, 429, 438, 445, 461, 482, 500, 558, 622, 664, 703, 724, 749, 820, 834, 847, 917, 936, 1034, 1128.
The World and the Chylde, 721.
Worthington, E. K., 518.
Wrecked, 812.

Yeats, W. B., 1, 12, 19, 29, 33, 36, 46, 61, 70, 72, 73, 76, 83, 87, 112, 116, 118, 128, 140, 143, 170, 172, 182, 199, 200, 205, 213, 215, 222, 229, 231, 235, 238, 240, 260, 261, 266, 267, 278, 282, 291, 297, 324, 330, 331, 349, 355, 356, 375, 380, 388, 397, 401, 423, 430, 451, 452, 459, 468, 479, 481, 499, 516, 525, 539, 597, 598, 605, 611, 613, 632, 635, 657, 674, 690, 717, 719, 727, 750, 758, 773, 776, 788, 791, 818, 821, 832, 845, 854, 891, 896, 911, 933, 941, 949, 958, 1025, 1027, 1056, 1145, 1160, 1162.

About the Compiler

NELSON O'CEALLAIGH RITSCHEL is an Instructor/Lecturer of English at Stonehill College. His essays on Irish literature have appeared in such journals as *LIT: Literature, Interpretation, Theory* and *New Hibernia Review* and the anthology *A Century of Irish Drama: Widening the Stage*.